AFTER PORNIFIED

Anne G. Sabo's outstanding book challenges us to rethink presumptions about porn, and to see it as varied and potentially progressive. It will be valuable to anyone who cares about images of women in the media, gender equality, and the role of film and television in our lives.

Andrew K. Nestingen, Ph.D., Associate Professor at the University of Washington and the author of *Crime and Fantasy in Scandinavia: Fiction, Film and Social Change* (University of Washington Press)

Anne G. Sabo offers one of the freshest and most articulate voices on the controversial issue of porn since feminists began hotly debating its virtues and consequences back in the eighties. A much-needed contribution to what has become a tired and predictable discussion, Sabo courageously brings new insight to an emotionally charged issue in a voice that is eloquent, reasoned and accessible to all. Her work will surely be respected for the rare understanding she brings to a completely new cultural phenomenon, one that most are unable or unwilling to take on: that of women creating their own unique pornographic vision and its implications and potential benefits to all.

Candida Royalle, iconic erotic film pioneer, entrepreneur, and the author of *How to Tell a Naked Man What to Do: Sex Advice from a Woman Who Knows* (Fireside)

At last a book that appreciates female directed porn as the important cultural phenomenon that it is. For decades the media has represented porn as being for men only and that any women involved in the industry are mere dupes. Anne G. Sabo explains why this is not only untrue (and always has been) but also that it is women who are moving the genre forward, both as directors and consumers.

Anna Span, Britain's first female porn director and the author of *Shoot Your Own Erotic Adult Home Movies* (Carleton Books)

Next to film professor Linda Williams, Anne G. Sabo is the most respected intellectual voice analyzing the new trend of feminist pornography. Actually Sabo's book demonstrates that it is not only a trend. Sabo shows that we are in front of a revolution of the genre.

Erika Lust, award-winning writer and erotic film director, and the author of *Good Porn: A Woman's Guide* (Seal Press)

One of the most remarked upon features of shifting production practices around porn and erotica is the growing participation of women. The presence of women was noted as a "significant trend in the industry" as long ago as 2000. However, there has been strikingly little attention paid in academic or more popular literature to women who make pornography. Books in both areas are very overdue so this book is very welcome. I think *After Pornified* will be of wide interest to women who already have an interest in the topic and those who know very little about it, and a good starting point for rethinking debates about women's relationship to porn.

Feona Attwood, Ph.D., Professor of Sex, Communication, and Culture at Sheffield Hallam University and the author of *Mainstreaming Sex: The Sexualization of Western Culture* (I. B. Tauris)

After Pornified does not cover the well-worn ground of whether or not porn should exist; instead Anne G. Sabo takes a close look at the kinds of sexually explicit material which are marketed as "for women." An analysis of these films which does not simply seek to criticize or dismiss porn for women by women is long overdue, bringing to the fore the political and personal intentions of a range of directors and producers, as well as the aesthetic and artistic considerations in making sexually arousing imagery. Written in an accessible style for an interested rather than an academic audience, *After Pornified* brings a much-needed dose of optimism to the debates about pornography, its content and effects.

Dr. Clarissa Smith, Reader in Sexual Cultures at the University of Sunderland and the author of *One for the Girls! The Pleasures and Practices of Reading Women's Porn* (Intellect)

After Pornified

How Women Are Transforming
Pornography & Why It
Really Matters

After Pornified

How Women Are Transforming
Pornography & Why It
Really Matters

Anne G. Sabo, Ph.D.

Winchester, UK
Washington, USA

First published by Zero Books, 2012
Zero Books is an imprint of John Hunt Publishing Ltd., Laurel House, Station Approach,
Alresford, Hants, SO24 9JH, UK
office1@jhpbooks.net
www.johnhuntpublishing.com
www.zero-books.net

For distributor details and how to order please visit the 'Ordering' section on our website.

ISBN: 978 1 78099 480 2

A CIP catalogue record for this book is available from the British Library.

The author has received financial support from the Non-fiction Literature Fund.

Cover image from "The Tunnel" on Candida Royalle's *Sensual Escape* (1988).

You may visit the author at annegsabo.com.

Design: Stuart Davies

Printed and bound by CPI Group (UK) Ltd, Croydon, CR0 4YY

We operate a distinctive and ethical publishing philosophy in all
areas of our business, from our global network of authors to
production and worldwide distribution.

CONTENTS

To Lilly and a future generation of empowered women.

Acknowledgements

This book has gone through many lives before turning into what it has become today, and several have helped sustain it through the process of me writing and re-writing it. Big thanks are due to all of you. To my colleagues at the Centre for Gender Research at the University of Oslo: What a wonderfully stimulating environment you provided me with while I was doing the first major chunk of research on which this book is based. To Terje Gammelsrud of Cupido: What a ride we had with the Good Porn event we organized and all leading up to it and after; I am thankful for our fruitful collaboration. To Linda Williams: Thank you for encouraging me to write the kind of book I wanted to write. I've returned many times to that sentiment. And to all of you who have listened, read, and given me feedback on earlier versions of this book: Thank you! In particular you, my dear friend and thoughtful reader Mary Madison. And Kristian Himmelstrup, Andrew Nestingen, Jennifer Severtsgaard, Daisy Christophersen, and my travel-through-life companion, lover and husband Leighton Hambrick to whom I also owe great thanks for his careful editing of some of this book's sections, and for ensuring I persevere. Special thanks to Marte Hult for generously lending me her meticulous copyediting services, in particular for this book's proposal with all its sample text. Thank you also Nancy Aarsvold and Diane LeBlanc for your advice and suggestions.

And lastly: Heartfelt thanks to all the women whose work I feature in this book. Thanks are due to several of you who provided me with copies of your films and kindly answered all my questions. Clearly, without your films, this book would not be. — Without your films I would not have envisioned this amazing potential of porn transformed to empower and inspire all women and men to stand up against a culture that discriminates, represses, contains, shames, and misrepresents women's and men's sexuality, all the while exploiting it. Your work has certainly encouraged me to take further charge of my body and self-image: to truly claim, own, enjoy and explore my body and sex on my terms. For that priceless gift: Thank you.

Introduction

How I Came to Porn

I never wanted to watch porn. When a former boyfriend years ago showed me some of his "glossier" porn, as he put it, I was completely grossed out. The premise of his porn was that all these Barbie-looking women would seek out a stud residing in this huge mansion, where he would provide them with their ultimate satisfaction by spraying his come all over them, which they in turn would greedily lick and smear all over their bodies. The cliché portrayal of yearning women in need of a man was in itself offensive to me. But it was especially the prolonged scene featuring the guy hosing down a group of women with his ejaculate that turned me off.

You'd think from our pornified culture that we all want porn. But we know that's not the case. Sure, women represent a large and growing audience for porn, representing at least a third of all consumers, adding up to millions of women watching porn each month.[1] But not everyone is crazy about what they see. Whether it's "high gloss" or amateur porn, in either case featuring deep throating women who are pumped hard, legs spread wide, all the while moaning for more with come-hither eyes. The stacks of mass-produced porn at seedy superstores off the interstate. Trashy hotel room porn. Online smut catering to any imaginable (and unconceivable!) fetish. And even "softcore" and "couples porn" allegedly improved to appeal to women, but not really. Plastic looks, porny music, bad acting, faked satisfaction.

But then I found something radically different.

What first got me turned on to the feminist potential of porn was actually my research on the literature of prosecuted freethinkers. Picture the poet/writer Christian played by Ewan

I

McGregor in Baz Luhrmann's movie *Moulin Rouge!* (2001): *fin-de-siècle* bohemians who believed in existential liberty and free love for all, women *and* men. Toulouse-Lautrec, whom Christian befriends in the film, has immortalized the sprit of the bohemian lifestyle through his artwork: posters and portraits of his friends at their many stomping grounds in Montmartre, the legendary artist neighborhood in Paris.

Cut to the US where free-love supporters were persecuted by the social purity campaigner Anthony Comstock. The editor of the free thought journal *Lucifer*, for instance, went to jail several times for publishing articles by women defending women's sexual freedom. A freedom that included the right to resist rape in marriage. These women free lovers were first wave feminists advocating sex education, the right to birth control, and the equal right for women to assert an active desire and make their own independent choices. Yet these women's writings were judged "obscene."

At the turn of the century in my native Norway, the women and men of the *Kristiania Bohème* were faced with similar acts of prosecution. I grew up in a country that has become known for its relaxed attitudes to nudity and most would add towards sex too. In fact, today's young women are described as a sexually liberated and empowered generation. Yet, a vocal group of young third wave feminists argue that a *"horny"* woman is still very much taboo. Obscene; too much. These women grabbed the media's attention recently with *Pink Prose: About Girls and Horniness*.[2] Writing from personal experiences, they reiterated a demand for women's equal right to assert an active desire. Modern women's so-called "sexual freedom" only goes so far, they argued. A woman is expected to be "sexual," but only so much. And also not too little. Balancing the speed limits of desire, she risks the labels of either whore or prude.

To this day, there are girls—and boys—who grow up in Norway feeling the pent-up weight of the Lutheran guilt about sex. I was one of them. I will never forget how my mom caught me red-handed one day, touching myself beneath the covers in my bedroom. The look of disapproval in her face. The humiliation I felt. I was maybe ten, and I was home sick from school. Later on my older sister gave me a book about sex and puberty. Still feeling the shame, I threw it to the back of my closet. I never looked at it again.

So I have always empathized with the bohemian free love advocates' desire to break free, existentially, socially, sexually. In the end, tracing their history led me to look into filmic porn again too.

Henry Miller's *Tropic of Cancer* has become legendary for its graphic depictions of sex. First printed in Paris in 1934 with financial backing from his lover Anaïs Nin, the novel was for years smuggled into the US where it was banned. Its publication in the US in 1961 led to a series of obscenity trials.

Around this time, two famed Norwegian authors also underwent lengthy legal proceedings because of the sexually explicit content of their writing: Agnar Mykle (*The Song about the Red Ruby*) and Jens Bjørneboe (*Without a Stitch*).[3] In the end, Miller was acquitted by the US Supreme Court, which declared his book a work of literature. Cut to Norway where Mykle was also exonerated by the Supreme Court of Norway, convinced of his novel's artistic merits. But not so Bjørneboe. Why? Because, decided the courts in the case of his book, its "literary value cannot be placed high" and "its edifying value is rather below zero."[4]

I have serious objections to this dismissive interpretation of Bjørneboe's text. As I have argued, it actually represents a clever take on the classic folktale, recognized for its socio-political anti-establishment undertones.[5] But what's even more troublesome about the courts' verdicts here are their failure to recognize the feminist quality of Bjørneboe's book as opposed to the misogynistic aspects of Mykle's novel. The latter focuses on the sexual exploits of the wannabe-free man Ask who takes then ditches a series of women in a desperate attempt to free himself from conservative norms. Bjørneboe's novel, on the other hand, portrays the empowered sexual journey of a young woman, Lilian. At first incapable of achieving orgasm due to a disabling sense of guilt, imagining what her mother and grandmother would think, she is helped by an orgasm specialist to overcome her feelings of shame and connect with her sexual self. Owning her sexuality, she then spends a summer backpacking through Europe where she celebrates a plurality of sexual encounters on consensual, mutual, social and gender democratic terms, including by participating in the making of a porn film. At the end of her journey, Lilian bemoans our culture's hypocrisy, permitting men to acquire the kind of "worldly experience" she has attained before settling down, but not so for women. Women who are judged by the very same men who've had their sexual escapades and who now preach from the moral high horse.

Caught up with the question of what constitutes art, the legal establishment failed to recognize any of this. Technically, it is still illegal to sell *Without a Stitch* in Norway, sentenced for not raising above the level of lowbrow culture to join the ranks of highbrow art. This prejudice against popular culture has meant that sexually explicit art house films featuring extreme sexual violence and rape, such as the French films *Baise-moi* (2000; by Virginie Despentes and Coralie Trinh Thi) and *Romance* (1999; by Catherine Breillat), have been allowed distribution and public screenings in Norway, but not so mainstream porn; not even new re-visioned feminist porn.[6]

The concept of re-visioned feminist porn was introduced to me by film scholar Linda Williams. Towards the end of her historical analysis of porn, *Hard Core: Power, Pleasure, and the "Frenzy of the Visible"* (1989), Williams discusses the potential of a *"re-vision* of hard core by women" as opposed to the "general revision" featured by the new lines of "cleaned up" "couples" porn. Williams borrows the term "re-vision" from recently deceased famous feminist poet Adrienne Rich. "The added hyphen," notes Williams, "suggests the revolutionary potential of 'the act of looking back, of seeing again with fresh eyes, of entering an old text from a new critical direction.'"[7]

Porn has traditionally been a "male genre," by men for men. In fact, as Williams points out, sex has historically been defined and discussed from men's point of view. Men are the ones who have speculated about women's sexuality; women have never had the opportunity to define it for themselves. If *re-vision* is for women within a male dominated economy "a necessary 'act of survival,' in order to be able to create at all," it is within porn, argues Williams, "that the idea of re-vision is most compelling: 'survival' here means transforming oneself from sexual object to sexual subject of representation."[8]

Candida Royalle's erotic Femme Productions films were a fresh concept at the time Williams wrote her book. And it is here Williams finds proof that *re-vision* and not just revision is possible; that women can seize the means of production to approach and portray sex on their terms and from their perspective, and not "from the viewpoint of the phallus."[9] Williams' careful close readings of some of Candida's early films made them come real to me. I was moved and inspired by what I saw. I wanted to see more.

What I have found are films that have empowered and inspired me. Films that feature women I can identify with. Mothers and daughters, single or partnered, younger and older, thinner or plumper. Women who confront culturally imposed sanctions regulating their behavior, and deeply felt issues shaping their lives. Women who reject the speed limits of desire enforced upon women. Women who refuse to be labeled.

Behind these films are educated women with high ideals and intriguing visions. Women who object to the discriminating portrayal of their sex in porn and popular media, and who speak up for women sexually and politically. Some of them stay clear of the "porn" word lest they turn their targeted audience away from their work. Instead they market their films as "adult," "explicit," "sensual," or "erotic." But others refuse to allow men free rein in defining porn, and therefore claim the "porn" word as a way to subversively change its meaning.

This position appeals the most to me. Because words can hold a lot of power.

Whore. Prude. Slut.

Women and men are cursed by words. And women and men have been cruelly labeled by words. In turn, some women and men have claimed words to deny their derogatory undertones.

"Porn" is a loaded word that brings up a lot of negative imageries in our pornified culture. "That's so 'porn'" has today become an expression to describe excessive or trashy taste. But imagine if the content and connotations, and even the effects of porn were different: positive and empowering rather than negative and degrading. That's what I've discovered to be the potential of re-visioned and transformed porn by women.

I have found that porn is not inherently bad; there has just been a lot of badly made porn. Postmodern sex-positive performance artist (and former "golden age" porn star) Annie Sprinkle is known for having said that "the answer to bad porn isn't no porn, it's more porn." I would second that but also insist that it strive to be better. And by that I am not referring to big production "high gloss," or "softcore," or "couples" porn. Or the mainstream porn industry's so-called lines of "women friendly" porn that do nothing more than gloss up the picture and soften the plot.

I am interested in the authentic porn made by women who show a sincere commitment to radically change porn, featuring female and male sexuality with respect and realism. Where porn becomes a vehicle for women to explore their own sexuality and define it for themselves. A new language, in fact not found

elsewhere, to talk about sex. A radically progressive and liberating gender democratic discourse with which to *think* and
approach heterosexuality. Presenting us with intriguing
openings of more room for women, as well as men, to explore
and expand our sexual play-field. In fact, new porn by women
shines the light on how we can all break free from confining
gender roles and erotic conventions, attaining fluidity,
democracy, and abundant space and possibilities in the ways we
encounter our sexual partners.

* * *

Over the years, I've come to spend a lot of time looking at
women's re-visioned porn. On research leave at the Centre for
Gender Research at the University of Oslo, I had the opportunity
to devote an entire year to just looking. When I first arrived in
the early fall of 2005, pornography was still censored, judged
"offensive" by Norwegian law. When Candida had some of her
porn sent to me from the US, it was confiscated by Norwegian
Customs and not released to me until I could prove I had
ordered the films for scholarly research.

The censorship of porn had, however, been the subject of
critique for years, despite the efforts of a small but vocal group
of anti-porn feminists. Then finally, in December 2005, the
Norwegian High Court ruled in favour of a porn magazine
editor accused of illegally distributing an uncensored issue of his
magazine. Essentially, the High Court concurred with the
defendant that the definition of "offensive" changes over time,
and in today's Norway, portraying "common" or "normal sexual
activity between consenting adults" can no longer be considered
"offensive."

The following spring, the Norwegian Media Authority (much
like the Motion Picture Association of America's Rating Board)
booked me as a consultant in the review of their guidelines for

handling porn. After a half-day workshop where I presented them with the criteria I have developed to qualify quality in porn, the Media Authority changed their policy for regulating porn to allow the distribution of previously censored porn. This means that it is now finally legal to distribute progressive feminist re-visioned porn by women, as well as other porn that portrays sex between consenting adults, including consensual BDSM.[10] Porn that depicts illegal acts of sex and violence, such as grave sexual coercion often featured in extreme bound and gagged porn, or sex with minors, animals, and dead bodies, remains illegal.

At the tail end of my research leave in Norway, I also led a highly attended and widely covered by the media event called "Good Porn" at a theater in downtown Oslo.[11] At the event, I talked about and showed clips from new progressive re-visioned porn. Joining me at the event's concluding panel were Barcelona-based feminist porn filmmaker Erika Lust and Britain's first female porn director Anna Span. Candida wished to join us but had a conflicting commitment. Williams, the Berkeley-based author of *Hard Core*, was one of the scholars attending the event.

This book is written as a continuation of the debate we sought to initiate with that event: about the potential of a new radically re-visioned and transformed form of porn and why it matters.

Whether you're into porn or turned off by it, I want to show you its potential. How it can empower, inspire, inform, and reform. How rather than leaving men in charge of the production of grossly discriminating porn that is leaking into the pornified representation of ourselves in advertisements and popular media, re-visioned porn by women is transforming porn as we know it. In fact becoming a real counterweight to the negative sexualization of women (and men!) perpetuated by the entertainment industry and all other porn.

* * *

High-profiled journalist Pamela Paul has devoted an entire book
to the subject of the pornification of our culture, with porn now
seemingly everywhere in our lives. In *Pornified: How Pornography
Is Damaging Our Lives, Our Relationships, and Our Families* (2005),
Paul belabors the many negative effects of porn beyond the
pornification of popular culture:

> Men who prefer the fantasy of porn to the reality of family
> life. Men who desensitized by what they see turn to ever more
> extreme porn. Men who feel their self-esteem crumble under
> the weight of shame.
>
> Hurt and jealous women who feel pressured to pony up.
> Women who feel expected to be ready for sex at any moment
> of the day and reach howling ecstasies within two minutes.
> Women who remark on the lack of foreplay from their porn-
> watching partners — men who instead push for oral sex, even
> when she doesn't feel like giving it.
>
> Sexualized children who grow up with warped ideas
> about sex. Children who emulate porn and pop stars by
> posting sexual pictures of themselves on the Internet.
> Children who act out porn scenarios with even younger kids.
>
> Intimacy disorders and relationships that crumble as trust
> is replaced by distrust and emotional isolation.[12]

I do not question that porn has an effect on us: quite the
opposite. But the porn that Paul refers to has nothing to do with
the porn that interests me. Concludes Paul:

> The sexual acts depicted in pornography are more about
> shame, humiliation, solitude, coldness, and degradation than
> they are about pleasure, intimacy, and love.[13]

None of this holds true for re-visioned and transformed porn by
women.

Re-visioned porn by women shows us sex that is pleasurable, intimate, and caring between women and men we can relate to. They meet their sexual partners on equal terms, and their sexual encounters—giving and receiving—are characterized by warmth and respect, and a mutual sense of adoration and affirmation. In contrast to the depressing porn Paul talks about, this kind of porn offers us heartening stories about real people as they enjoy and explore their sexualities; providing us and our partners with helpful ideas and inspiration for our sexual lives.

As a matter of fact, re-visioned porn by women presents the kind of positive thinking about sexuality and instructive role modeling of healthy sexual behavior that I would want my daughter to be exposed to as a part of her sex education when she grows up.

The great thing about porn affecting us is that it can actually have a positive effect on us. Re-visioned porn proves my point. Re-visioned and transformed porn can change the way we think about and practice sex in positive ways, just as porn up until now has affected the way we picture and practice sex in negative ways.

I want to show you this. And because too many porn debates are based on assumptions about what porn is all about; and because porn critics and anti-porn activists tend to hijack the media with shocking tales of the porn industry's abuse of women and the revolting things they are made to do for the camera, I am going to visualize the films for you so you can see for yourself.

A Note to the Reader

My film presentations trace the history of women's re-visioned and transformed porn, which begins with erotic filmmaker Candida Royalle. A pioneer within the re-visioned porn by women movement, she has produced eighteen films since the launch in 1984 of her company Femme Productions. In 2006, she was presented with a Lifetime Achievement Award at the inaugural Feminist Porn Awards. Candida is still an active voice within the women's progressive porn movement, creating her own films and now also mentoring a new generation of female filmmakers, including for her new subdivision of films Femme Chocolat, which promises to deliver films featuring a more ethnically diverse cast of actors and actresses, directed by women of color.

I devote all of Chapter 1 to Candida's films. In fact, I spend more time discussing her work than I do on any other single filmmaker featured in this book. There are two reasons for this. Firstly, Candida has gained an iconic stature within the re-visioned porn by women movement; among audiences, the adult industry, academics, and sex educators and therapists who commend her films' positive sexual role modeling. Second, I use her films to establish the criteria with which I qualify the quality of all the films I look at in this book. As you will see, Candida's films—most of which follow a feature film format—stand out for their progressive content, communicating a genuine concern to empower women (and men!) to overcome personal and cultural sexual issues and to explore their sexuality; and with their high cinematic quality, featuring stunning soundtracks. I round off Chapter 1 by summarizing my set of criteria, broken down according to content and style.

It took nearly two decades before Candida was joined by another woman establishing her own independent film company with the intent of radically re-visioning porn from a female perspective. However, in the late 90s, the mainstream motion picture company of famous Danish film director Lars von Trier launched a line of feature film porn aimed at women, Puzzy Power, with von Trier's international producer Lene Børglum at the helm. Chapter 2 is about these films, which represent a *positive* mainstreaming of porn where mainstream goes porn out of a recognized need for a new progressive, gender democratic kind of porn.

All the Puzzy Power films feature the kind of production values you would expect from a well-established film production company and reflect a sincere intention to feature women as agents of their sexuality. Nevertheless, a couple of the films suggest the power of patriarchal conventions; a tradition from whose grip it can be a challenge to liberate our sexual fantasies. Instead of dismissing these films, I spend some time on them because they actually teach us a few powerful lessons to keep in mind as we proceed with re-visioned porn. And when progressive content in line with Scandinavia's long tradition in promoting gender equality and women's rights is complemented with high cinematic quality, the result can be excellent, as I also show. As a whole, with its reassuring ties to an established motion picture company, Puzzy Power has helped a growing audience of women approach re-visioned porn to see its potential, and it has done a tremendous job in removing some of the stigmas around porn for women that in the past have prevented it from flourishing.

The movement of new re-visioned porn by women saw a growth spurt after the turn of the millennium and has really only gained momentum in the last few years. The remaining chapters are about these re-visioned porn films made by a growing number of women. I devote a separate Chapter 3 to one of them: Anna Span who brands herself as Great Britain's first female porn director. Anna has since 2003 released twenty DVDs under her

Easy on the Eye label; most form part of her "Anna Span's Diary" series. She is the first to measure up to Candida in terms of sheer production volume. However, whereas Candida and the Puzzy Power directors pay careful attention to esthetics, Anna makes serial based porn that focuses less on making it artistic and more on capturing steamy sex. Some of her porn is shot gonzo style: a documentary approach to shooting where the cameraperson— here Anna—is present in the action, visibly and audibly engaging with the characters. In fact, in terms of format and sexual content, Anna's porn resembles mainstream porn more so than any of the other films I look at in my book.

That said; there is much that sets Anna's porn apart. For one, her porn features a new generation of confident women who will not let the sex be over until they are satisfied. And their actual orgasms are convincingly captured: the hectic flushing spreading around the neck as they approach, the shivering quivers over face and body when they come. Anna's porn also stands out with its charming incorporation of humor, both to capture chemistry between the characters, and also in a hilarious Benny Hill sort of way that charges the scenes while at the same time being highly entertaining.

In Chapter 4, I present the new porn Candida has collaborated on with a new generation of young women concerned with sexual politics and empowerment. I also look at the re-visioned porn made by a couple of gender bending hip sex-positive New Yorkers. And I look briefly at the Libido Films made by a couple of Chicago-based academics.

I devote more time to the films of German-born Great Britain-based Petra Joy whose "art-core" porn stands out with its creative commitment to a fluid feel of intimacy and sensuality. Candida recently made available under her Femme Productions label one of Petra's films. Of her own accord, Petra arranged a competition for which she solicited entries from up-and-coming women from around the world, encouraging them to create their own alternative porn. She then collected and produced the top entries. I look more closely as the woman who won the first prize; the Australian Louise Lush, also known as Ms. Naughty. Louise began making her own "vanilla sex" erotic films only recently, but as the Webmistress behind the largest domain network of porn aimed at women, Ms. Naughty has produced online porn for more than a decade. A former librarian and freelance journalist, she has built a reputation for herself as an educated feminist sex- and porn blogger who objects to double standards and cultural hypocrisy.

I move on in Chapter 5 to look at the stunning erotic music video porn films made today by women who are highly skilled in design. Candida actually introduced the "erotic rock video" format with her first two Femme Productions collections. Today, it is revitalized and modernized by women with a fresh perspective and a new artistic edge. They are situated in Europe where they benefit from a greater openness to sex and progressive porn, as well as more support for the arts. With backgrounds ranging from fashion, design and media art, they collaborate with upscale design companies and see their work featured at reputable film festivals and even prestigious art institutes.

Finally, in Chapter 6, I look at select re-visioned porn films that stand out especially for their compelling cinematic qualities. Additional testimony to the *positive* mainstreaming of progressive porn as first represented by Puzzy Power, and today also evidenced by those involved in creating artistic music video porn, re-visioned and transformed cinematic porn is fronted by famous filmmakers and artists. Their films—often bracketed with art house sex films—are shown at coveted film festivals, including Cannes. In particularly inspiring is the government sponsorship a group of women in Sweden recently received for the production of their feminist porn. When the news reached the ears of Conan O'Brien, he made a sketch about how "only in

Sweden" does the state give away tax money to support new porn. For now, O'Brien might be right. But this may very well change as more eyes are opened to the potential of feminist porn.

As you proceed with your reading, you will see that I have my close reading-viewing of each film marked off to highlight the visual experience. I hope this will make it easier for you to return to specific films and that it can help open up a space for the film viewing experiences within my overall discussion of the films and the women behind them.

As a quick and easy reference, I include below a list of all the films featured in the following. In the Appendix, you will also find a list of all the featured porn producers' websites. I also include a list of female-run and women-oriented sex shops that sell new porn by women in the Appendix, and a list of progressive film festivals that feature new re-visioned porn by women.

The Films

Listed in the Order Discussed

Chapter 1: From Candida Royalle's Femme Productions

"TV Idol" (on *Femme*, 1985), "Kamikaze" and "Freight Elevator" (both on *Urban Heat*, 1985), "The Tunnel" and "Fortune Smiles" (both on *Sensual Escape*, 1988), "The Pick-up (on *A Taste of Ambrosia*, 1987), "Shady Madonna" and "In Search of the Ultimate Sexual Experience" (both on *Rites of Passion*, 1988), *My Surrender* (1996), *The Bridal Shower* (1997), *Three Daughters* (1987), *Eyes of Desire* (1998), *Revelations* (1992)

Chapter 2: From Zentropa's Puzzy Power

Constance (1998), *Pink Prison* (1999), *All About Anna* (2005)

Chapter 3: From Anna Span's Easy on the Eye Productions

"Supply Nurse," "Sperm Sample" (both on *A & O Department*, 2004), *Be My Toy Boy* (2009), "Head to Toe Service" (on *Good Service*, 2003), "Holloway Rd. Market," "Columbia Road Market, London, E2," "The Cut, Waterloo, London SE1" (all on *Pound a Punnet*, 2003), "Shoot the Slut" (on *Play the Slut*, 2004), "China Chelsea," "Neil Down for Joy" (both on *Anna's Mates*, 2004), *Women Love Porn* (2009)

Chapter 4:
From Jamye Waxman

Under the Covers (2006; in collaboration with Candida Royalle and her Femme Productions), *Personal Touch* (2007; three-part series), *101 Positions for Lovers* (2009)

From Abiola Abrams for Candida Royalle's Femme Chocolat

AfroDite Superstar (2007; in collaboration with Candida Royalle)

From Tristan Taormino's Smart Ass Productions
The Ultimate Guide to Anal Sex for Women I and II (1999, 2001), *House of Ass* (2006), *Chemistry* (4 vols. released since 2006), *Expert Guide to Sex* (15 vols. since 2007), *Rough Sex* (4 vols. since 2009), *Expert Guide to Pegging: Strap-on Anal Sex for Couples* (2012)

From Marianna Beck and Jack Hafferkamp's Libido Films
Ecstatic Moments (1999), *Urban Friction* (2002), *Trial Run: Adventures in Romance* (2007)

From Audacia Ray
The Bi Apple (2007)

From Petra Joy (formerly of Strawberry Seductress)
Feeling It! Not Faking It... (2008), *Her Porn* (3 vols. since 2009), *Female Fantasies* (2006), *Sexual Sushi* (2004), *The Female Voyeur* (2011),

From Louise Lush's Indigo Lush
That's What I Like (2009), *Paddling the Pink Canoe* (2009), *Fucking Is The Only Prayer* (2011), *The Thought Of Her* (2011, short film), *I.M. In Love* (2012), *The Thought Of Her* (2012, long length)

Chapter 5:
From Erika Lust's Lust Films & Publications
The Good Girl (2006), *Five Hot Stories for Her* (2007), *Life, Love, Lust* (2010), "Handcuffs" and "Love Me Like You Hate Me" (both on *Life, Love, Lust*), *Barcelona Sex Project* (2008), *Cabaret Desire* (2011), "Room 33" (on *Cabaret Desire*)

From Murielle Scherre's La Fille d'O
J'fais du porno et j'aime ça (2009; I make porn and I love it)

From Eva Midgley for Coco de Mer
Honey and Bunny (2004), *Erotic Moments Collection* (2008), *Peep Show* (2009)

Chapter 6:
From Anna Brownfield's Poison Apple Productions and Hungry Films
The Money Shot (2002), *The Band* (2009)

From Jennifer Lyon Bell's Blue Artichoke Films
Headshot (2006), *Matinée* (2009), *Skin. Like. Sun.* (2009; in collaboration with Murielle Scherre)

From Ovidie
Orgie en noir (2000; Orgy in black; in collaboration with Marc Dorcel), *Lilith* (2001; produced by Marc Dorcel), *Histoires de sexe(s)* (2009; in collaboration with Jack Tyler for French Lover TV)

From Sophie Bramly's SoFilles Productions
From *X-femmes* (2008) and *X-femmes 2* (2009):
  "Pour Elle" (2009; For Her), "Samedi Soir" (2009; Saturday Night), "Peep Show Heroes" (2008), "A Ses Pieds" (2008; At Her Feet), "Vous Désirez?" (2008; You Wanted Something?), "Le Beau Sexe" (2009; The Good Sex)

From Mia Engberg
Come Together (2006), *Dirty Diaries* (2009)

Chapter 1

Femme: A Woman's Perspective
in the United States

When Candida Royalle (b. 1950) entered the realm of porn, it was just about to come into itself, having evolved from the late 1890s stag films. Alfred Kinsey's reports on sexuality in the 1940s and 50s had begun to scratch away on the cultural seal silencing a diversity of sexual behavior in women and men. In the 60s, select movie theaters showed films that purported to "document" sex in faraway liberal places, like Scandinavia where Denmark became the first country in the world to legalize porn in 1969.[1] The softcore film *Without a Stitch*, based on Jens Bjørneboe's book, was among these popular Scandinavian sex films.[2] The uncensored version of the film opened in January 1970 in New York at Loew's flagship theatre on Broadway, and crowds streamed in to see it. Later, hardcore films allegedly reporting on Denmark's pornography industry paved the way for actual hard core to be made and screened in the US too.

The term "porno chic" came out of this era in the early seventies when ambitious directors like Gerard Damiano (*Deep Throat*, 1972) and Radley Metzger (*The Opening of Misty Beethoven*, 1975) set out to merge pornography with mainstream feature film. San Francisco—home to the summer of love when almost one hundred thousand aspiring hippies flocked to the Haight-Ashbury neighborhood in 1967, with neighboring Castro becoming the sanctuary for homosexuals across the world—became their haven.

It was also where Candida, a native New Yorker, sought refuge in the early seventies. While a student at Parsons School of Design and City University of New York in the late sixties and early seventies, she became actively engaged in what was then a growing feminist movement, attending consciousness-raising workshops in the Bronx and organizing clinics where local women could come for free PAP smears and pelvic exams. But as the movement became increasingly radical, the intoxicated feeling of sisterhood waned and she felt herself less at home:

> I remember feeling that I was becoming a minority; that I was not sticking to the party line because I did have a boyfriend, and it was kind of like I was sleeping with the enemy. There was a real move to rejecting heterosexual relationships and embracing lesbianism, or embracing separatism.[3]

The sisterhood unraveled with activist and writer Robin Morgan (b. 1941)—famous for the statement that "pornography is the theory, and rape the practice"[4]—taking the lead of the radical anti-men, anti-sex feminists in New York. In 1972, Candida left for San Francisco.

The daughter of a professional jazz drummer, Candida had also studied music and dance. In San Francisco, she performed in jazz clubs and with avant-garde theater troupes. Having been schooled in the art of figure drawing from nude models at Parsons School of Design, and coming of age during the sexual revolution, posing and performing in the nude didn't seem far-fetched.

Candida recounts making about five or six features a year for about five years, working "with directors who took pride in what they were doing," and avoiding "the sleazebags who were contemptuous of their casts." However, she adds, she did not like "the often crude depiction of sex in most mainstream porn." Experiencing a "gnawing ambivalence" about her work, she returned to New York in 1979 and quit making films after about a year.[5]

Back home in New York, Candida would meet on a regular basis with other women who were also former golden age porn actresses—Annie Sprinkle, Veronica Hart, Gloria Leonard, Veronica Vera, Kelly Nichols, and Sue Nero—serving as a support group for each other. They called themselves "Club 90" after the address of Sprinkle's Manhattan apartment on 90 Lexington Ave where they'd meet. In January 1984, the women performed a consciousness-raising theater piece modeled after their meetings titled *Deep Inside Porn Stars*. Gathered on a stage made to look like Sprinkle's living room, they chat over tea and cookies, revealing themselves as quite ordinary women.[6] Hart was a new mom at the time and brought a baby doll onto the stage to represent her son Christopher. The audience overhears childhood memories and stories about the women's first sexual encounters—all typical.

But most importantly, the "porn stars" talk about how working in porn has affected them. And they discuss the business of porn; how it stereotypes and discriminates against women. Introducing a new sex-positive feminist viewpoint, they refuse, however, to be labeled victims or dismissed as stupid. Instead they call for a revolutionary feminization of the industry and a porn that would not discriminate against women or represent their sexuality in misleading ways.

That same year, Candida, with the financial support of her Swedish in-laws,[7] founded Femme Productions with just this in mind. Explains Candida on her decision to produce her own films:

I began to wonder what it would be like to create explicit movies that give us good information about sex while entertaining and inspiring us. Could I create movies that accurately reflected female desire, movies that women and men could enjoy together? I *didn't like* a lot of what I saw in contemporary porn, but rather than march around waving banners of protest, I decided to put my money where my mouth is and try to produce adult movies that make us feel good about ourselves. After all, people are not going to stop looking at sex, and if women don't take control of the means of production, men will continue to do it for us, continuing to erroneously define female sexuality.[8]

The advent of VCR in the late seventies signaled the demise of porno chic and the arrival of cheaply mass-produced porn. However, the more affordable means of production also allowed someone with a more modest budget like Candida the opportunity to create her own alternative explicit films defining female sexuality on her terms. Comments Candida:

I created the Femme line to give adult movies a woman's voice and explore what we women desire and want from sex. Adult entertainment up until now has been the sole domain of male desire and inclination. Now that women are seeking out equally fulfilling experiences in the bedroom, we're eager to explore erotic entertainment and to create a sexual language of our own.[9]

Today, Candida's films are often marketed as feminist pornography. But personally, Candida maintains a preference for "erotic" because, as she explains on her web pages, porn has come to mean a certain kind of depiction of sex, conjuring up "images for many women that are distasteful" and which do not agree with how she portrays it in her films. As Candida points out:

Having been the first filmmaker to try and appeal to women viewers, calling my work porn was likely to turn them off before they even gave it a chance and took a peak! Calling my work erotica or adult entertainment seemed more accurate and more productive in terms of marketing.[10]

Among the negative images many women associate with porn is the so-called "money shot," capturing the man's external ejaculation, usually on a woman's face, chest, belly or butt, and always to her great satisfaction; often she'll lick it greedily. Originally mainstream filmmakers' slang for the image that cost the most money to produce, the phrase was subsequently appropriated by the pornography industry where producers pay the actors extra for this shot, the idea being that the "money shot" is what sells; what the audience wants to see. Also known as the "cum" or "come shot," the "money shot" has, as Williams points out, become a leitmotif of the porn genre since the seventies.[11] It is described by British-born college professor Gail Dines—who is among today's most outspoken porn critics—as "one of the most degrading acts in porn," marking the woman as "used goods."[12] It was definitely an image that turned me off and against porn when I first saw it.

But more than refraining from the "money shot" to turn down the gross factor and appeal to more women the way it's done by softcore and so-called "couples" porn makers today, Candida has, from the making of her first film, been radically re-visioning what porn is all about, including as a workplace. Anti-porn critics often assume that women who're led to porn are sexual abuse victims and drug addicts. That they are poor and uneducated and see no better alternative than sex work. That they are sexually violated and discriminated against on a daily basis. Shelly Lubben, the former American porn star turned Christian anti-porn activist, feeds into this kind of thinking. Writes Lubben in her memoir:

I put on a good show but I never liked performing tricks in the sex circus and preferred spending time with Jack Daniels rather than the male performers I was paid to fake it with. That's right, none of us hot blondes enjoy making porn. In fact, we hate it. We hate spreading our legs for sexually diseased men. We hate being degraded with their foul smells and sweaty bodies. Some women hate it so much that I would hear them vomiting in the bathroom between scenes. I would find others outside, smoking endless chains of Marlboro Lights.[13]

Most of Candida's actresses, however, are "high-minded career gals who are often juggling postgraduate studies alongside their sexual hijinks," as she puts it to the Melbourne-based newspaper *The Age*.[14] She prefers to work with actual couples or actors who have sex with each other also off the set, and she strives to ensure a sense of intimate space for the performers even as they're being filmed having sex, allowing time and care with the making of each individual scene. No one is ever asked to do anything she or he is not comfortable with. An advocate for safe sex, Candida insists the performers have proof of negative HIV status before the filming begins. And condoms are always used unless the actors are a real-life couple, clear of the virus.

To *The Age* Candida also touches on some of the problems she has with the content of mainstream porn. She points out its "misogynous predictability" of "formula" based scenes that are shot "to show things as grotesque and graphically as possible" ("cunnilingus looks like open-heart surgery and "the 'money shot' is always the external 'come shot'—it's like your typical bad sex—no imagination and it's always over when the man comes"). Her goal, continues Candida, is to remind people that "the whole body is an erogenous zone." Her films are not "goal oriented" towards a final "money shot;" instead, her films depict sexual activity within the broader context of women's emotional and social lives.

At her website, Candida has further described her films as follows:

I define the Femme line as "sensuously explicit" adult erotic movies that women can relate to and share with their partners. My movies feature high production values, non-formulaic eroticism sans the gynecological close-ups and obligatory "money shots," and attractive people who are more realistic, varied in age and body type, who genuinely relate to each other with passion and sensitivity. I try to create characters with personalities and real lives and relationships, and make every effort to hire actors and actresses who can stay in character once the sex starts rather than reverting back to being porn stars and studs.[15]

I find Candida's description truthful. Her films stand out both in content and style. And whereas the soundtracks in mainstream porn are often caricatured for their monotonous pumping beat, the soundtracks in Candida's films are carefully composed to match the ebb and flow of the characters' desire and pleasure. Candida compares the composition of a soundtrack that can accompany a fifteen to twenty minutes long sex number with the composition of a symphony with different movements. Among the accomplished musicians who have composed soundtracks for her films, is the late jazz saxophonist Gary Windo of the Gary Windo Quartet. Windo also played for Pink Floyd and The Psychedelic Furs, one of England's most popular post punk bands.

Candida used the music video, which had come into prominence only three years before with the launch of MTV, as the format for the short films on her first two collections, *Femme* (1985) and *Urban Heat* (1985), marketed as "erotic rock videos for couples."[16] While also avoiding potentially stiff lines by porn performers without much acting experience, the rock video format illustrates how effective music can be in communicating the development and intensity of desire and pleasure when the soundtrack matches what we see.

At their best these fifteen to twenty minutes long erotic rock videos present the audience with a sexual dance where bodies come together in a harmonized flow in which neither is more or less active or passive. Among my favorites is "TV Idol" on *Femme*, which portrays the masturbation fantasy of a young woman.

The film begins with a picture of her. She's in her early twenties, dressed in a long pajamas T-shirt, tennis-socks, and a bandana around her head along the lines of fashion at that time, and lying casually on a bed draped with a well-worn velvety red blanket. The lights are dimmed; she's watching television.

All of a sudden the man from the show she's been watching is in her room. He looks kind and handsome with his head covered by dark blond wavy hair. The camera rests on him while he, looking intently at her, begins to take off his clothes, sitting down on her bed when she sits up to help him.

The camera focuses in on his firm buttocks as she pulls down his briefs, slowly, capturing his hips in profile; her breasts just barely touching his stomach. His penis rises up towards her as she gets his briefs off.

An electronic dissonance has charged the picture from the moment he entered her room. Now suddenly for a moment silence fills the picture until the music picks up again ever so gently, only tentative strokes on the piano at first, then more confident, an almost rocking but also titillating melody as the two now come together. She caresses his penis; he strokes and licks her breast.

The camera continuously captures the two bodies in profile, creating the image that neither one of them is above or beneath, but both on the same level. She lies down, pulling him with her, but his body is not on top of hers. Rather their bodies are intertwined, with her legs wrapped around him. The camera closes in on them in floating extreme close-ups: the softness of skin, the curve of a thigh, her foot, a leg around him, his hips. The camera continues like this in a constant flow, caressingly and democratically without prioritizing either body or body part.

Close-ups of their faces capture the intensity of the pleasure they sense while the music fills with an intense modernistic dissonance, as if from a distorted voice: soaring pleasure enters the piano melody. His face contorts with pleasure; she closes her eyes and turns inward, feeling her face with her hands. Through fervent thrusting and massaging of her breast, the dissonance escalates until their flesh shivers in ecstasy, their entire bodies tightly strung bows, melting in the last contractions.

At last a few quiet piano strokes after a silent pause. His body a spoon around hers as he kisses her gently; she smiles, running her fingers through his hair, and he smiles back. Wrapped around one another, the two hold each other with their bodies and eyes.

A non-objectifying gaze

Except when eyes are closed and the sensation turns inwards, the two characters in "TV Idol" hold each other continuously with their eyes. What I find striking about the way the two look at each other, is the *exchange* of a desiring gaze while the camera for its part refuses to objectify either one. Instead "objectification" here becomes an affirming, adoring act.

The two characters' mutual exchange of an adoring gaze also emphasizes the gender equal quality of their sexual encounter. The position of the camera is a factor here. Even when he at first is standing while she's lying down in bed, the camera frames the two in a way that gives the impression of the two being on the same level. The camera does not look down at her from his point of view or up at him from hers—it focuses instead on the shared space between them. The closer their two bodies, the closer the camera moves to their shared space, always proportionally attentive to the both of them.

The significance of the camera's position and how it frames the characters bodies will become even clearer if we compare this film with an average mainstream porn film like the German *Feuchte Tagträume* (Wet Daydreams) by Philippe Soine. This DVD was distributed in 2006, though as is the case with a lot of mass-produced porn, the year of production is not listed on the cover or in the credits. In contrast to Candida's democratic filming, Soine shoots from the male perspective and uses a series of high and low angles to signify the power difference between the man and woman.

The first episode shows the daydream of the presumably Italian lifeguard "Marco" getting laid by his female German colleague. In the first shot, he's removing a plastic tarp covering the pool while in voiceover he begins to daydream back to the day he got laid by her. A picture of her fades in over his dreaming gaze. She's at the other end of the pool, treading on an elliptical machine. She's wearing an orange bikini, the color glaring against the pale background, white concrete walls and chlorine water. The camera zooms in on her, lingering on her empty stare, then her incessantly treading feet, before tilting up to capture her legs, this angle making them look longer. The picture narrows in on her butt; she's wearing a thong bikini bottom, her buttocks moving up and down along with her monotonous treading that makes a dull repetitive sound, which is accompanied by a thumping synthesizer rhythm.

In the next shot the camera has moved to capture her from the front, focusing on her breasts before rolling over them and up along her shoulders and neck to her face. There is nothing glamorous about her, despite her stuck-up pose with her chin tilted out a little, her lips pouting. She has a fairly large freckled nose, her skin blemished, blue-gray eyes. Her hair is a bland washed out blond in a feather cut that looks dated with long bangs covering her left eye.

After an abrupt cut (in voiceover Marco explains that he has in the meantime mustered the guts to approach her during one of their breaks), we see the woman in a white swimsuit in the pool on her way out of it, up along the ladder. The camera looks down on her from the perspective of the lifeguard at the top of the stairs. His hand enters the picture from the top left corner with his index finger pointing down on her breasts: "give me your clothes," he commands with a heavy German accent. "Get in the water and give me your clothes." She says something in response, but his voice drowns out most of it. She stumbles a little on the ladder on her way down again into the pool where she begins to undress, her look somewhat bewildered. Fumbling with her straps, she attempts a smile.

In voiceover the young woman explains that she's been lusting for her Italian colleague for a while, but has lacked the courage to take the initiative. Though in this way verbally reassuring the audience, however, she becomes visually increasingly submissive as the camera moves up and away from her. When his penis enters the picture from the top left corner, it looks bigger than she does to the right of the screen.

Marco starts to jerk off with his left hand—we hear him moaning—while she continues to undress down in the pool, blinking with big eyes up at his huge hard dick with another attempt at an awkward smile. He lets go of his dick and waves her up to him while repeating, "give me your clothes." She hands him the white swimsuit, which he hurls behind him. It gives a wet smacking sound when it lands on the hard tiles. "Come!" he commands her as a male rapper on the monotonous soundtrack pounds out; "yo, this is a really funky beat, I want you to check it out, 'cause it goes something like this: duh, duh, tack, uh. — Check this shit out!" The rapper's and the lifeguard's voices blend into an oozing raw testosterone that fills the picture.

The young woman really has no other way to go; behind her is the pale chlorine blue water, the tiles on the bottom of the pool a dirty white grid. She gets up the ladder, her genitals cleanly shaved, looking almost childlike. She lifts her eyebrows, her eyes open wide when she gets closer to his dick; she jerks her head back a little, but he quickly grabs it, grasping a wad of her hair and pulling her hard towards his crotch while shoving his dick in her face. "Come!" he says again, "Sit!" He gets her down into a kneeling position that can't be comfortable, her little smile gone; she looks dead serious. But in voiceover she continues to reassure us in German: "I'm not very good in English, but now I understood what he wanted from me: a real good blowjob." Presumably, she has no wish to resist. But when he begins to smack her face with his dick from side to side, she closes her eyes.

Aside from the opening scene where we see Marco uncovering the pool, the camera continues to focus primarily on the object of his daydream throughout the episode. The episode concludes after fifteen minutes with him coming, standing as she sits, spraying his sperm down and into her mouth in a typical "money shot."

Clearly, there are a lot of factors that separate *Feuchte Tagträume* from "TV Idol"—from the sex to the sets, the sound and lighting quality (or lack thereof), the performers' body language (regardless of the lines they speak), and the ultimate "money shot." But what interests me in particular when comparing these two films is how manifest the significance of the camera's placement becomes when considering the issue of "objectification" and the level of gender equality. Specifically: what the camera captures of the characters; and from which or whose angle and perspective. Take for instance the introduction of the penis:

In "TV Idol," where the camera captures the bodies of the two equally and proportionally, on the same level throughout, his penis is seen as rising up to greet her when she pulls down his briefs, as both sit on their knees in bed together. As we saw in the *Feuchte Tagträume* episode, on the other hand, the lifeguard's penis appears in fact larger than all of her when it enters the picture from the top left corner of the frame where he's standing by the pool: his cock a commanding rod above her head with her down to the right in the pool.

"Objectification" is typically used to describe something negative; a discriminating fixation on body parts that reduces the subject into an object. This is certainly the case in the "wet daydream" where the camera obsessively focuses on her butt, boobs, and pussy from his perspective, and where she is cast as the object of his demand. In "female friendly porn" then, one might expect to see women as the actively doing subjects and not first and foremost gazed at objects of men. But this approach fails to consider a notable attribute of the gaze: its quality of *devotedness* by which someone can experience really being seen and affirmed.

"TV Idol" captures such devotion. The woman and man hold one another through a mutual exchange of a desiring gaze, as well as by an intertwining of their arms and legs. In this way "TV Idol" is able to portray intercourse as a gender equal act. It is not he who "takes" her, or her him in reverse. Instead the two encounter each other on the same level as an integrated interlacement of bodies in continuous roll-around flow.

A new democratic sexual discourse

"TV Idol" presents us with a gender democratic experience of a sexual encounter. In this way "TV Idol" gives us a new language with which to talk about sex; a language which breaks away from the male perspective that has dominated the way we talk about sex up until now, featuring a male active subject and a female passive object. This is important, for as Williams points out, sex has historically been defined and discussed from men's point of view (Williams here refers to Michel Foucault's historical analysis of such discourses), as is evident when we consider erotic and pornographic material throughout the centuries. Men are the ones who have speculated about women's sexuality; women have never had the opportunity to define it for themselves.[17]

Sex-positive feminists have since the sixties and seventies fought to take ownership of their sexuality and define it on their terms. We need assertive narratives about women who are sexual on their own terms and not purely on men's conditions. But beyond that, I envision an equilibrium where neither women nor men feel the need to prove their power. "TV Idol" shows me that it is in fact possible to portray sex in a way that is neither male dominated nor female dictated but egalitarian.

This is also important because feminists have for decades struggled with the tendency of erotic fantasies to play on power inequalities. Robin Morgan, for instance, writes in *Going Too Far: The Personal Chronicle of a Feminist* (1977) that she felt like she "'capitulated' ... like an alcoholic gone back to the bottle" when she fell back on her erotic fantasies after she had wilfully decided to stop fantasizing, since she could only be sexually stimulated by fantasies in which she was dominated, fantasies she considered symptomatic of "patriarchal heterosexuality."[18] In purportedly gender equal Norway, third wave feminist and journalist Martine Aurdal (b. 1978) recently wrote about the numerous times she's caught herself in a role-play right before orgasm, reminded by "an annoying voice in her head" that the power relations the role-play is based on stem from gender roles from the stone age.[19]

> The opening episode of Candida's *Urban Heat* (1985) also shows how sexual encounters between women and men can be envisioned in a more gender democratic way; where, to quote Williams, "the performers use their bodies as dancers do, acting out for their mutual benefit."[20] Produced in 1984, the same year as Madonna released her album "Like a Virgin," there is also something very charmingly eighties about this film, from the characters' dance style to their outfits, hairdos, and make-up. Candida got the idea for the film at a screening party held at a New York dance club called Kamikaze (since closed): the bartenders and waitresses started telling her how they would sneak off to the back room for sex, and that she should do a movie about that.
>
> In fact filmed at Kamikaze, the opening shot shows people dancing to an upbeat disco song. (Candida had a friend of hers compose the soundtrack for this erotic rock video: Jorge Havana (Socarras), vocalist for the then hip

New York band Indoor Life. And she sang the vocals for this soundtrack with him.) The camera scans the crowded space, but keeps returning to a petite waitress with blond curly hair and one of the bartenders. She giggles to something he says to her with a little smile. A couple on the dance floor also receive a lot of attention: she with short spiky hair and a thick black band painted over one of her eyes; he in wide parachute pants and a shortcut tight fitting T-shirt, baring his midriff. His way of dancing stands out in its stylized pantomime-like style.

The waitress and the bartender escape the scene, heading down the stairs to the storage room in the basement. They smile, kiss and make out; undressing each other and having sex leaning against a table stacked with gin and whiskey bottles. Filters are added in post-production, giving the scene an animated artistic look. The camera keeps crosscutting between the couple in the basement and people on the dance floor above, in particular to that one specific couple—we can hear the music equally well both places: "Dancing!" urges the choir insistently.

The couple dancing eventually depart into their own world and the dance floor becomes empty around them as they move in a trancelike dance, their bodies melting together. As the two downstairs begin to dress, the clothes on the couple above drop to the floor. The camera circles the two in dreamy shots and movements as they spin around on the empty dance floor, the sex a part of their dance.

Another episode on *Urban Heat* that has since received a lot of scholarly attention shows a more mature woman seducing a young man in a freight elevator. The episode was used in a study by Dr. Ellen Laan, a psychologist at the University of Amsterdam where she had a group of women watch this episode and then also a scene from a typical mainstream porn film. The women's sexual responses were monitored while they watched the scenes, and afterwards they were interviewed about their reactions to them. None of the women knew anything about who made these films. The measurements of the women's physical arousal showed that "the women responded equally—and powerfully— to both clips," but the women "reported being annoyed, repulsed, disgusted and decidedly not turned on" by the mainstream porn film, "while they said they were excited, amused and aroused" by Candida's film.[21]

Williams points out how in this episode too the focus is on what *entire bodies* are doing for one another—"bodies performing pleasurably for each other"—and not primarily on the male sexual organ, which "does perform, finally, but not as the climax or end of the action. Even when the elevator bell rings and the couple hurriedly dress, the final fade-out shows them beginning to rub up against each other again."[22] In other words, the female initiative and desire this film portrays refuse to be held back by either her age or his performance. Comments Candida about this film:

> It's gone on to become a favorite for women both for its portrayal of a woman who's in charge of her sexuality, and because it features a "mature" woman who's attractive and comfortable with herself. In a genre that seems to endlessly drive home the idea that only young perfect-bodied women are sexually desirable, it's a welcome relief to see a woman of age and substance set a scene on fire![23]

The half-hour film "The Tunnel" on *Sensual Escape* (1988) is another powerful example of female sexual agency visualized by

Candida. This time it's the journey of a somewhat repressed younger woman, however; a woman who in the end manages to surmount her personal problems and take charge of her sexuality. As an early example of Candida's feminist commitment to empower women to overcome sexual issues—be they the result of psychological histories or cultural codes—the film suggests why she has since received such fabulous recognition from sexologists and therapists. The film is also intriguing for the new symbolic language it presents to feature sex from a woman's point of view.

In "The Tunnel" the erect penis and "money shot" are replaced as the central symbols for the sexual agent and his climax with an alternative symbolic to portray the *woman* as the active, desiring sexual subject—across railings, out of a net, through a membrane—and *her* pleasure, flowing through a multifaceted ecstasy; in itself a departure from the stereotypical depiction of women's orgasm in mainstream porn where an ultimate escalation in screaming moans is typically meant to represent the woman's definite orgasm.

"The Tunnel" is about a young female artist who is constantly bothered by the same dream where she sees herself in an abandoned tunnel decorated with lush velvety blankets, dimly lit by a huge chandelier in the ceiling and torches burning along the walls (the film was shot in a former New York night club called The Tunnel, which originally served as a depot for trains). At the end of the tracks is a stage on top of which a man—naked except for a white cloth draped around his loins—is dancing erotically for her to a seductive pulsating rhythm while stretching his arms out towards her (the abovementioned jazz saxophonist Gary Windo composed the soundtrack for this film together with rock musician Don Preston).

The film begins with one of these dreams. At first all we see are the railroad tracks, the camera sliding over them on a dolly to a hypnotizing synthesizer music. Then the screen is filled with a picture of her, captured in profile, draped in a long, flowing translucent material, her dark wavy hair cascading down her back. She stands firmly grounded, but is looking back towards him on the stage, slowly moving his hips, side to side. Pictures of her, him, or both, and the tracks, begin to dissolve into one another in a dreamy flow. Or the camera cuts abruptly and quickly in a shimmer of shots, revealing glimpses of a black spiderweb bodysuit beneath the loose material draping her. The camera dwells on the man, gliding over his naked thigh, hips, an elbow, arms and hands, which he is reaching out towards her, his shoulder, a collarbone.

The music expands with higher pitched chords, the heartfelt urgent blows from a saxophone, and the choiring of a siren. And now she begins to walk up towards him, accepting his invitation. He kneels down before her and begins to pull off her gown before the film abruptly cuts to a surrealistic image of her behind a violet membrane, revealing only the contours of her face, nose, lips and hands that are trying to break through it.

She startles with a gasp and sits up, and we see her in a sun lit studio apartment in pajamas on a mattress on the floor.

"The Tunnel" alternates between this dream scenario where she at times sees herself on the stage with him, her back arched in pleasure, until she's suddenly trapped behind the membrane again, or running away but getting nowhere—and everyday episodes where we get to know this young woman better; how awkward she feels around men, never finding any chemistry. How she returns to her easel and sketches she's made of the man from her dream, faceless, at the end of the tunnel.

In the concluding part of the film, the dream scenario merges with her actually entering a tunnel to visit a man she met in a park and who presented himself to her as a massage therapist who works with clients' pent-up tensions. Through a constant use of dissolving images where one picture fades out as another fades in, dream shots are used in this sequence to emphasize the erotic, and to highlight the woman as the active subject advancing towards the man, over tracks and up to the stage where he has set up a massage table draped with burgundy red blankets. Here she lets desire and pleasure burst through, over and over again, through the spiderweb suit, and finally the membrane too.

The entire massage sequence is about her pleasure. Shots pasted on top of each other give the impression that she's being massaged and stroked by an abundant amount of gliding hands, massaging, stroking, licking, sucking, and fingering her. She does not return the favor at the end. This is her session, a penis is never seen; he keeps all his clothes on.

The focus on female desire and pleasure in "The Tunnel" underscores Candida's feminist commitment to empower women sexually and portray their sexuality truthfully. As we've seen, this is a commitment shared by her friends in "Club 90." After founding her company, Candida invited each of them to write and direct a short film, which she compiled and produced as three videos under the banner "Star Directors Series." "The Tunnel" is a part of this series.

The short films the "Club 90" girlfriends made attest to the women's desire for an honest and respectful portrayal of women's, and men's, sexuality in porn, addressing sexual insecurities and featuring realistic scenarios.

"Fortune Smiles" by Gloria Leonard (also on *Sensual Escape*) is about a man and a woman (played by a young Nina Hartley, who remains a famous outspoken sex-positive porn star), both divorced with children; the two have been dating for a while.

We see them first at a restaurant, it's Friday night, she tells her date that her ex has their son over the weekend; he suggests take-out at her place instead of staying at the restaurant. Cut to her living room, leftovers of Chinese food on the table, as we listen in on their silent thoughts and worries while they flirt and chat. She's afraid he'll notice her stretch marks, he feels silly with a condom in his pocket and wonders if she's uptight about oral sex. She is horny, but wonders if she should take it easy so he doesn't think she's too forward in bed, but she doesn't want him to think she's a prude either. Despite their insecurities, there's a comfortable intimacy between the two, and after they've had sex, they confess their insecurities to each other.

"The Pick-up" by Veronica Hart on *A Taste of Ambrosia* (1987) is about a married couple with children who maintain the spark in their sex life by pretending to be strangers who meet at night on the street before they head home to "his" apartment to have sex. "Shady Madonna," on the other hand, by Veronica Vera, shows how sickly a Christian fanatic's puritanical repression of sexual desire can be. Annie Sprinkle's "In Search of the Ultimate Sexual Experience," portrays Sprinkle's own sexual journey from uninspired sex on the couch with trashy porn on the TV playing in the background to new age tantric sex (both on *Rites of Passion*, 1988).

To role-play your way free

Several of Candida's films portray role-play along the lines of

Hart's "The Pick-up." In her sex guide *How to Tell a Naked Man What to Do: Sex Advice from a Woman Who Knows* (2004), Candida reflects on the liberating and therapeutic potential of acting out different scenarios and roles, and rotating the roles. Her feature film *My Surrender* (1996) is built around different couples' erotic fantasies where role-play serves a central function. The film's main character is a professional and discrete photographer, April, who facilitates the making of private couples' own little porn videos of which they themselves are the stars. After reviewing their video recorded requests, April invites couples to her studio where they perform their favorite erotic fantasies for her camera. The fantasy of a successful attorney, for instance, whose husband works for the government, is to play the part of "the naughty school girl" with her husband acting as a certain "Professor *Sir*" who must punish her with a good spanking. A middle class woman, on the other hand, wishes to take on the character of a sexy glamorous pornographer completely in charge of the situation as a male porn actor—performed by her husband— auditions for her.

What's interesting to me about both these women's fantasies is their reflective play on clichés; the women mindfully appropriate and play with stereotypical fantasies without becoming reduced to the part they perform. On the contrary, role-play becomes a way to expand the characters' sexual play-field.

My Surrender also features role-play as a therapeutic method of processing personal issues. In an electrically charged mastur- bation scene featuring April at the mercy of Robert, an architect she met at an opening, we see that her fantasy is to surrender control. However, she is struggling to let go of her defenses. In a video message she records to Robert, she explains that her many rejections of him since the night they met are based on fears about all the anger and disappointments to which getting involved with another person can lead. She talks about how tired she is of hearing men tell her they can't make her happy, no matter what they do, because they're right: We're not each other's mom and dad who can "kiss it and make it all better."

Candida further explains on the film's extra material that April's wish to surrender the wounded child inside and love as an adult had been a real issue for her when she wrote the manuscript for this film: she had just broken up with a man with whom she'd been together for a couple of years, and it had been a hurtful break-up. Candida often shares personal experiences and life lessons this way, both in her book and on her DVDs' extra material, which always include a video "Message from Candida" where she emphasizes her desire to create films that will not merely entertain people, but that can also be helpful with good information and creative ideas. Describing her films as "edutainment," Candida stresses that each of her films is purposely made to convey *meaning*. In her book, she recalls "reading an interview with the director Ingmar Bergman, in which he said, 'If you have nothing to say, you shouldn't make a movie.'" "I imagine we'd have a lot fewer movies and a lot less schlock on the video shelves if everyone adhered to that message," concludes Candida.[24]

Since many of Candida's films focus on helping people overcome issues that affect their sexual lives and relationships, sexologists and therapists have often used them in their practice. Her films have also been shown in conjunction with the conferences of, among others, the American Psychiatric Association (APA), and the American Association of Sex Educators, Counselors, and Therapists (AASECT), of which she is the first producer of adult films to be accepted as a member.

In *The Bridal Shower* (1997), one of Candida's more pronounced pedagogical films, advice and directions on how to deal with sexual complexes and perk up one's sexual life—in particular through role-play—are shared by a group of friends, mature professional women, primarily with careers in health care. They have gathered at the home of Penny to celebrate the upcoming wedding of their youngest friend, Claire. While Claire is opening her gifts—satin sheets, a black teddy, and a basket full of sex toys, massage oil, and even a porn film (one by Candida)—the women recount their favorite fantasies and steps they've implemented to improve their sexual lives, captured in erotically charged and esthetically well-shot flashbacks.

Sandy explains how she got Eric, her young Italian lover, to slow down when they had sex by bringing him along on a picnic for some erotic food play in the lush countryside, spreading her feast on him and then his on herself. Before things moved on, he had to take his time licking his plate clean, so to speak.

Dorothy describes her experiences with Jeremy whom she met five years after her husband passed away. After the loss of her husband, she had lived a celibate life, raising her son and studying medicine. But when she met Jeremy, she was definitely ready for sex again. He, on the other hand, had in the two years since he got divorced had an awkward sexual experience, which had left him afraid that he suffered from erectile dysfunction. After reading about what she could do to help him with his performance anxiety, Dorothy arranged a private poolside date where the focus would be on arousing Jeremy so much that erection would be of no doubt, several times, without taking it any further. Masters & Johnson originally developed this so-called "give and get" method, which Candida comments on both in her book and on this film's commentary.

Laura talks about how long it took before she was able to let go of her fear that her husband Brad would judge her weird if she shared her fantasy with him about being blindfolded — "to be at the mercy." Penny jumps in, remembering how long it took her before she was able to tell her husband Jack how she prefers to "get head," getting over that "good girl-bad girl shit, and yes, even good girls like sex." Laura recounts how a course on human sexuality, which she took while studying for her Master's in social work, helped her realize that fantasizing is good for people's sex lives. And then, "when Brad and I felt comfortable enough to open up and tell each other our fantasies, it really brought us closer together." Her flashback scene captures both their personal intimacy and the electric tension of being blindfolded for the first time. The scene ends with a "next time it's your turn" invitation to Brad.

When Claire pulls out the porn film from the basket, she's pleased to see that it's "even one that I'll like!" Laura asks if it doesn't bother her that her fiancé Raul gets turned on by watching other women, but Claire explains that she doesn't think it's so much the women as such but what they *do* that turns him on. "That's a really interesting way to look at it!" comments Penny; "I always felt really threatened by all those perfect women." "Penny! With that gorgeous bod' of yours?" Dorothy interrupts. "Well, all I ever hear from Jack lately is how beautiful this one is, and how sexy that one is," replies Penny. Claire: "Oh yeah? Well, you should hear how Raul talks about you, Penny." "Me?!" interjects Penny. Claire: "Whenever one of those girl-girl or group scenes comes on, he says he pretends it's you and me."

"Really?! And it doesn't bother you?" Penny asks. "At first it did," Claire responds, "but he makes me feel like the most desirable woman in the world. Besides, I think you're pretty hot too," she adds with a little smile. "Whoa, a little bi-action here?" Sandy teases. "Don't knock it till you try it," Claire answers with a big smile. "So, tell me more," Penny says, adjusting in her chair before Claire begins to describe one of her and Raul's favorite fantasies; a hot threesome in their wooden kitchen, imbued with the warm glow of sunrays and sizzling pots, to which Penny is invited for some food and sex play.

Penny's immediate reaction to this fantasy is that it's "hotter" than anything she'd ever considered doing. To which Dorothy breaks in with a "Come on girl, get to work!" Which, replies Penny, is the problem; after ten years of marriage, it feels like "work." The women find out that Penny recently discovered a checked ticket to a striptease club in Jack's pocket, which, considering how their relationship has been suffering lately, really upset her.

Penny's friends determine to help her. Their plan is to get Penny to give Jack what he wants: a striptease show, this one starring Penny. Penny refuses at first, but the friends egg her on. Claire offers to teach Penny some of her "moves." "Raul loves it when I strip for him," she smiles. Laura thinks she might have some ideas too, since she supported herself while completing her Master's degree by stripping. Dorothy also chimes in, as does Sandy who trained for years in ballet and jazz dance, and eventually Penny gives in.

The women have a lot of giggly fun together, trying out sexy lingerie and practicing different moves. In the film's concluding scene, Jack comes home to an empty candle lit living room with instructions to sit down in front of the TV. Which he does, watching the women's homemade video before Penny enters the room for her star performance in which she gives him his very own personal striptease show.

Her role-play serves as successful foreplay. They have sex on the sofa, she comes before him, and they embrace after he's come too. We see an old photo of the two on the mantelpiece before the picture fades out. On voiceover we hear Penny on the phone with Claire, thanking her because the celebration of Claire's impending marriage has saved her own: she and Jack have just had their best sex in years!

One of the things I like the most about *The Bridal Shower* is its realism. At the onset, the characters are not all in modern sexually exploring and gender equal relationships. But they are confident mature women with a great deal of awareness about who they are and how they work with their partners. They strike me as being genuinely concerned with personal and relational growth. While attractive looking, none of them abide by the unrealistic standards with which the media—and mainstream porn—constantly bombard us. Only Nina Hartley (who plays Penny) has had her breasts done.

I also like how this film features more mature women and men. A major new study conducted on behalf of the UK Film Council found that mature and older women feel marginalized in film.[25] These women are eager to see film roles for women that more accurately communicate the characteristics of the modern, sexually liberated mature and older woman rather than being cast as background, sexless figures. The majority also felt that mature women were generally under-represented in films and that younger women were glamorized. By featuring a diverse range of women in terms of age and body type, Candida addresses the concerns of these women where the big screen and popular media fail them.

Another film that illustrates Candida's efforts to empower women, regardless of their age, is *Three Daughters* (1987). This film was selected by AASECT for a special screening at one of its national conferences due to its "positive sexual role modeling." The film features an upper middle-class family when all the grown daughters are home one summer before the youngest takes off for college. The film portrays the sexual lives of the daughters, as well as of the mother—performed by veteran porn actress Gloria Leonard (b. 1940). Wearing a loose dress to cover some added pounds, she rekindles her sexual love life with her husband when they are left alone in the attic in anticipation of having the house to themselves again.

Three Daughters' portrayal of the youngest daughter's sexual awakening is also interesting. In one scene we see her lying in bed studying a classic Betty Dodson book with illustrations of female anatomy while examining her own with a hand mirror, before drifting off into masturbating.[26] After this, she also explores sex together with a girlfriend before having her first sexual intercourse with a man.

Eyes of Desire (1998) features another kind of sexual awakening, this one involving the use of a telescope. The film focuses on the quiet photographer Lisa who is taking a break from her relationship with boyfriend Jamie by staying at the apartment of her friend Amy who, in the meantime, is staying with her boyfriend Tim. The film's premise is that Amy has a telescope in her living room, which she uses to look at her boyfriend in the building across from hers. This is an erotic game the two play together; he also has a telescope directed at her apartment so that they can "perform for each other." In the film's opening sequence, Amy leaves an impish invitation hanging in the air before leaving: to take a peek around eight when Tim comes home.

Lisa is a seeking person but shy, as she explains to her more boisterous and sexually adventuresome friend. Craving space and time away from her boyfriend, we get the sense that Lisa's relationship with him has failed for quite a while to give her what she's seeking. A professional photographer (we often see her studying slides), she is even considering a job offer that would involve a significant move.

What I like best about *Eyes of Desire* is how it is capable of capturing Lisa's inner quandaries through the combination of a tantalizing soundtrack and the focus on the gaze; how the pleasure in *watching* is underscored.

Cut to that same evening: Lisa is sitting with her legs curled up on the couch with a book in her lap, the living room dark aside from a lamp on the side table and flames from the fireplace. She looks at the clock: five to eight. She continues to read. Looks at the clock again. Hears the echo of Amy's words. In the end, she gets up, goes to the telescope; and puts her eye to the glass. A close-up freezes her eye in the dark as the sound of a tentative melody begins to play; vibrating tones from a synthesizer with tickling piano strokes on top. Then dead silence. She withdraws from the telescope, reluctant to continue. But soon her eye is back, and she gets to see more; we get to see more. Dark shots of Lisa in the living room, looking through the telescope, and the warm light in the rooms she looks in on and the action there, charged with the vibrating tones. Another dead silence, and she steps back again. Wavers. But then again the tickling piano strokes enter and, sighing as if exasperated with herself, she rests her eye on the telescope's glass. Through it we see a blur of unfocused images as the telescope scans buildings and windows over the dark abyss between them until she finds

Tim's apartment; all to the quivering vibration in the music that grows ever more intense.

Torn, Lisa continues to look in the days that follow. Day and night. And into more homes than Tim's and the teasing sexual role-play and hot sex she watches take place there between Tim and Amy who casts knowing glances in the direction of her own apartment. One night she comes across the role-play of a couple getting ready for a party. First the man: in front of the bedroom mirror, wearing a silver shining dress. Enter the woman. Upset that he has put on a similar dress to the one she's in, and not a tux as the invitation called for, they begin to argue. She blames him for ruining her underwear, which he has also put on, to which he replies that she seems to like it since she's getting wet. The exchange ensues in laughter and steamy sex. When cuddling afterwards, she giggly reassures him that in the future he may borrow whatever he'd like from her.

Eventually Lisa realizes that she's being watched too. She finds a telescope directed at her and discerns the contours of a man in his window. We see the flickers from the white in his eyes as he watches her, she who has been watching others and who eventually accepts the invitation to pose, strip, and touch herself for his eyes.

The film doesn't end here, but continues to develop the tension between the two, first over the phone and ultimately in person. In *Eyes of Desire 2* (1999), Lisa's sexual exploration takes the shape of an even more fearless experimentation with various lusts and fetishes.

Political activism: The right to see

Advocating an empowered sexual exploration and a reflective use of role-play, the *Eyes of Desire* films are interesting both for their featuring of role-play as a way to expand the characters' sexual play-field and explore their sexualities, and also for the point they make about the gaze. In particular the pleasure in watching (scopophilia)—specifically in a sexual context (voyeurism)—and also in being watched, sexually.

As the board member and co-founder of Feminists for Free Expressions (founded in 1992), Candida has been committed to fighting political and cultural censorship throughout her career. In *Revelations* (1992), perhaps her biggest investment (and in fact shot on 35 mm), she portrays an authoritarian regime's censorship of all art and eroticism, and how deadly such repression can be. Candida made the film in the early 90s, outraged by the government's anti-porn measures instigated by the disputed "Meese Report" of the Attorney General's Commission on Pornography. Appointed by President Reagan and dominated by conservatives, the Meese Commission concluded that "pornography is degrading to women," and asserted a causal, though in fact unproven, link between porn and violence, essentially reiterating Robin Morgan's slogan: "Pornography is the theory; rape is the practice."[27] As Williams points out, the Meese Commission failed, however, to define pornography beyond one Associate Justice's statement that "I know it when I see it."[28] This left all sexually explicit films vulnerable to the government's prosecution.

In December 2005, Candida re-released *Revelations* on DVD with expanded extra material as a reminder that the battle against censorship is not over. That same year, Republican Senator Sam Brownback, acting as the Chair of the Senate's Subcommittee on the Constitution, Civil Rights and Property Rights, had led a series of hearings on pornography. Arguing that porn is "morally repugnant and offensive" and "harmful to its users and their families," Senator Brownback even asked legal experts if the courts might be moved to whittle away at First Amendment rights in the face of a public health crisis.[29]

Revelations explores what life would be like in a society where its citizens have been deprived the freedom to express themselves sensually, creatively, and emotionally; where sex is only allowed for procreation; where everyone wears shapeless gray overalls, inhabiting sterile apartments; where one risks being arrested for keeping art.

As the opening credits scroll over the screen, fearlessly announcing the names of the actors and crew involved in the production of the film up front, softly lit images of a couple making love float over the screen before the film abruptly cuts to an extreme close-up of a woman's face, framing only her eyes. In contrast to the soft red light used in the shots of the lovers, the lighting here is harsh, revealing the skin's lines and blemishes. Pointing to the film's theme about what is allowed to be seen or not, the shot insists on her inherent right to see while also indicating her vision's imprisonment, both through the restricted framing and also from her questions to the viewer: "Did I tell you how I ended up here?" "How orderly things are outside?"

The camera then cuts to the outside as she, Ariel, begins to tell her story. We see military people in uniforms beating citizens in overalls, barbed wire-fences and factories in the background, the sun barely visible behind the smog. Everything from the uniforms to boxes and containers are marked with the regime's emblem; an "N" for the "new order" that has the crescent shaped blade of a scythe attached to each end. Symbols in general — from bedrails to symbolize the forbidden nature of sex for pleasure, to the American flag blowing in the wind with birds soaring into the sky to represent freedom—play a central role in *Revelations*, which makes good sense; in a time of censorship, language must be camouflaged.

Then we see Ariel one morning as she leaves a drab looking apartment building to pick up the day's provisions. A voice calls out from a megaphone, announcing that house-to-house searches will be conducted in order to root out all "decadence and subversion." When Ariel returns to her apartment building, her neighbor—wearing only his baggy underwear—is taken away by the security police. For a moment he fixes his eyes on her, imprinting an insistent stare, which overwhelms her with curiosity that ultimately causes her to enter his apartment.

In sharp contrast to the film's other shots of exterior and interior spaces, the walls in her neighbor's apartment are covered with playful and colorful Miro'esque drawings. Searching for something that might be of use to her in his pantry, knowing that most people who are taken away never return, Ariel finds the door to a narrow secret backroom, barely bigger than a closet, with erotic pictures on the walls, and in the back a TV with a VCR and a stack of erotic videos, revealing to her a sexuality of a sensual passionate kind of which her life is void.

Inspired by what she sees, Ariel begins to experiment with colors in her kitchen, splashing tomato sauce on the colorless curtains and walls. And she attempts to introduce sensuality and pleasure to the cot she shares with her cold husband only to be rejected. In the end she gets arrested while masturbating in the backroom of her neighbor's apartment while watching an erotic video.

> Imprisoned in the film's concluding scene she tenaciously
> claims ownership of what she has seen; pictures and stories
> that remain with her.

Revelations is a powerful film that arouses political activism, as
well as sexual stimulation inspired by the erotic porn films,
which were shot on High 8, giving them the authentic grainy look
of video. Cinematically, the film stands out too, bearing
testimony to the laborious attention Candida devoted to every
detail in this film's making. Candida recruited the woman who
plays Ariel (Amy Rapp) from mainstream motion pictures; she
had no previous experience in porn.

What makes this porn so good: Summary of Criteria

It is Candida's attention to cinematic quality as well as her commitment to a progressive sexual politics that make her films so good. These two main criteria of design and content can be further broken up into more specific sub criteria that can be used to qualify what makes any porn film more or less good:

1. High cinematic production value
   - *The acting is strong and convincing.*
   - *The manuscript builds the sex into a realistic context.*
   - *The settings and costumes are realistic.*
   - *The musical soundtrack complements and even adds to what we see;*
     the sighing is truthful and balanced as opposed to the exaggerated moaning we hear in mainstream porn.
   - *The lighting supplements the atmosphere.*
   - *The picture quality presents what we see esthetically.*
   - *The cinematography and directing is done by someone with a good eye for the right shots, settings, and frames.*
   - *The editing is done by someone with an eye for good cuts and transitions, splicing the right shots for best effect.*

2. Progressive sexual-political commitment
   - *The camera shots, angles, and movements capture and frame the bodies and their sexual encounters democratically, presenting a new language for gender democratic heterosexuality.*
   - *The film presents us with a gender democratic gaze of devoted mutuality as opposed to the objectifying gaze of the woman in traditional mainstream porn.*
   - *The film legitimizes consensual voyeurism and affirms the satis-faction in being seen, as well as the pleasure in seeing (scopophilia).*
   - *The film illustrates the use of a subversive role-play, critically*

appropriating, revising, and playing with erotic fantasies.

- *The film suggests an alternative symbolic to portray sexual agency, desire, and pleasure than the mainstream porn's focus on erection and money shot.*
- *The film confronts political censorship and the historical baggage of guilt and shame around sex.*
- *In line with social and political trends, the film portrays a society with increased gender equality, including a growing specter of diverse forms of intimacy, where women and men have a larger play-field to practice their sexuality, but where sexual taboos linger and narrow gender categories continue to confine the experience of gender and sexuality for many.*

While of course each film I discuss in this book doesn't address all of the criteria, they are consistent in an effort to re-vision porn, as we shall see.

Chapter 2

Puzzy Power: Mainstream Goes Porn in Scandinavia

The high budget Puzzy Power line of porn is often referred to as an example of the kind of porn women like to see. Launched by Scandinavia's largest motion picture production company Zentropa of the famous Dogme film director Lars von Trier,[1] with von Trier's international producer Lene Børglum (b. 1961) at the helm, these feature porn films have helped remove the ick factor from porn for a growing audience of women. A widely prize-awarded director, in particular at Cannes Film Festival, and never afraid to provoke controversy, von Trier recently announced that he too intends to direct his first sexually explicit film this year.

Lene told me more about the background for Puzzy Power when I met with her at Zentropa's large studio complex just outside of Copenhagen. In the late 80s and early 90s, Lene participated in the experiential art house underground film movement surrounding the notoriously transgressive filmmaker Richard Kern in New York, creating 8 mm loop films that show explicit sex in fragmented shots while seeking to push out of, and troubling up the boundaries of conventional norms and definitions for gender and sexuality. These films were the inspiration for Puzzy Power. But, added Lene, it took some jokes from her colleague Peter Aalbæk Jensen, who co-founded Zentropa with von Trier, to get her started. For years, she said, and especially at Cannes press conferences, Jensen would tease her for her former background in "porn," an allusion to Lene's sexually explicit 8 mm loop films. Then one day, she decided to take him up on it and give porn a shot, but with an esthetic inspired by the 8 mm loop films, and with content that would appeal to women. She asked her collaborator from the underground film movement, the aging but still noteworthy queer activist Knud Vesterskov (b. 1942), to plot out a manuscript and direct the first film.

At the same time Lene invited a group of women—including a film producer, a porn model, a sexologist, and an editor for an erotic magazine catering to women—to join her for lunch to discuss what kind of porn women might like. Their conversation resulted in the composition of a manifesto (von Trier's "Dogme 95 Manifesto" was an inspiring, fresh concept at the time)[2] for the kind of porn women might like to see and according to which the films were to be made. The women's "Puzzy Power manifesto" emphasizes the significance of plot to explain the sex "so we can relate to the characters and what goes on between them. It is not enough for four unknown actors to enter stage right, drop their pants and simply get down to it." Further, the films must "be based on women's pleasure and desire," focusing on "feelings, passions, sensuality, intimacy, and the lead-up." The beauty of the body, both male and female, must be emphasized, and not just genitalia. Subtle humor is welcome. The films can be set in the past or present time. Banned are scenes where women are subjected to violence or coercion, and especially "the oral sex scene where the woman is coerced to perform fellatio, her hair pulled hard, and come is squirted into her face." However, "it is fully acceptable to film female fantasies in which the woman is raped/assaulted by an anonymous man/a bit of rough trade, or if it is clear from the plot that what we are seeing is a woman living out her fantasy, perhaps by agreement with her significant other."[3]

Rococo extravaganza

I would say that all the Puzzy Power films fulfill the guidelines of the manifesto. However, of the three Puzzy Power feature films that up to now have been released, I consider only *Pink Prison* (1999) as truly successful with respect both to cinematic quality and to upholding a progressive sexual-political commitment. And not Knud's *Constance* (1998), which I was surprised to find so stereotypical, especially in light of Knud's experience within queer and art house underground film—having made several intriguing films where traditional gender roles are shattered to create fluidity, democracy, and abundant space and possibilities in the ways in which the bodies of women and men meet. What instead interests me the most about *Constance* is what it reveals about the power of traditions and stereotypes that can interfere with an intended re-vision of porn.

Constance illustrates the points made by feminist film scholar Laura Mulvey in her classic critique from 1975, "Visual Pleasure and Narrative Cinema." Along the lines of the Madonna-whore dichotomy, Mulvey argues that the woman's traditional function in film has been to arouse either desire or dread, playing either the part of one who must be helped or punished. *Constance* and also *All About Anna* (2005), the third and so far final Puzzy Power film, feature these dichotomous female roles, despite the filmmakers' better intentions. In fact, when I met over coffee with one of the two women who wrote the manuscript for *All About Anna*, I realized that she had envisioned a much more complex main character than the stereotypical woman the film ultimately brings us. And she was not the only one involved in the film's making to agree on this.

Knud also presented me with all good intentions when I met with him over tea in his apartment on a groggy Sunday morning. But after showing me several clips from his many gender bending transgressive, sexually explicit films, he sat back in his kitchen chair and told me he felt that in porn for women he couldn't take the same subversive approach to traditional gender roles as his starting point in the way he has done in his queer and underground films. Perhaps thinking that he had better give women what they're used to getting, not fully seeing the subversive potential of re-visioned porn, or questioning the limits of remaking—at what point is it no longer porn?—Knud's film in the end offers more of a revision of porn than a radical revision. In any case, the idea for *Constance*, he told me, was to cast a sexually experienced woman (performed by an experienced porn actress with silicon breasts) together with a sexually inexperienced woman (performed by a young slender woman with no former experience in porn) and use that as the starting point for the film's dynamic.

Despite the film's dichotomous portrayal of women's sexuality, *Constance* is certainly an improvement on mainstream porn, striving to show women as agents of their sexuality. It also focuses more on female desire and pleasure than mainstream porn. Many of the actors, in particular the title character Constance performed by Anaïs aka Sabina S. (b. 1978), avoid the stereotypical porn look while still being very attractive.

I met with Sabina on a chilly spring day in a quaint coffee shop in Copenhagen. At the time she was working on a Bachelor's degree in pedagogy. Off to see some friends after finishing her hot chocolate, she brought along her pet Freya, a ferret who stayed in her lap as we talked.

I connected with Sabina as the afternoon hours rolled by. She talked about her desire to combine her interests in sexuality and pedagogy working with children, developing and promoting a better and more comprehensive human sexuality education program for youth. And she talked about the need for more openness around sex, including sexual experimentation and fetishes, and also towards new alternative porn. She had not played in any other alternative or feminist porn films after *Constance* thought she told me she would have liked to, but not with all the prejudices that linger around porn. She said she's afraid acting in even feminist porn would make it difficult for her to practice as a pedagogue. That is also why she did not want me to use her last name. However, she spoke enthusiastically about the exciting pioneer feeling at the set during the filming of

Constance: the safe atmosphere; the health measures, including HIV testing and use of condoms; the good working arrangements; and the slow pace, recording only one scene a day.

I found it striking that a young woman who resides in the country that first legalized porn—a country that has become known for its liberal attitudes to sex, porn, and even prostitution—worries about social stigmas with respect to porn. In response to which Sabina talked to me about the absence of a Danish sex-positive feminism along the lines of Annie Sprinkle's as a counterweight to what she described as a conservative organization of anti-porn feminists, much like its Norwegian sister organization with which I had become quite familiar: the abovementioned small but vocal group of anti-porn feminists who for more than two decades have fought tooth and nail to maintain a censorship against porn, arguing that all porn is inherently violent and degrading against women.

Constance is set in the past; the settings a mixture of gothic and rococo. The premise is that a modern young woman has found the diary of her great-grandmother Constance. The opening shot establishes her reading it. The diary takes us back to Constance's time and her sexual journey with only brief crosscuts to the woman reading in the garden.

The first shots of Constance captures her chasing through an overgrown cemetery surrounded by flames late at night, dressed in a loose white gown, soft brown curls around her face. Filmed in slow motion, the shots allude to her internal struggle. In voiceover we hear her:

I am Constance. Follow me. Help me. Everything is aflame. ... I know ... everyone knows. When the world is on fire and ... you are afire with longing and desire,

---

you have to spite the dangers to find Lola's house. Everyone knows and whispers about it. In Lolas house you can learn everything. In Lola's house, desires are the law and life.

The film crosscuts to Lola in her salon, lounging on a violet rococo sofa, dressed in a green brocade dress, eating a cherry as if having sex with it. And now we see that she is in fact being licked; she arches her head in pleasure, gliding further down on the sofa. In close-up we see her vulva, the swollen labia that a young man dressed in a white cotton shirt is licking, sucking, and nipping with his lips. She takes another cherry, using it to play with him and herself, marking her position as the one in control. He is her young sex slave, Paw, serving her with his eyes closed, apparently content with his lot.

There are more crosscuts between a chasing, seeking Constance outside and a lounging, relishing Lola inside; the camera cuts if possible even closer to her shining vulva, revealing its folds and creases. Paw licks and kisses her greedily, sinking his head deep into her flesh. Licking her lips, Lola sits up and has him get down onto the floor on all four; he's naked except for his nightshirt. She pulls up his shirt and the camera circles around his buttocks, which she strokes and lightly spanks, further emphasizing her power over him.

A flurried Constance knocks on the door and Lola— annoyed by the interruption—receives her at the door, giving her new guest her immediate attention when she sees the state she is in. The music softens. Paw sits down in a rococo chair opposite the sofa where the two women sit, Constance resting her head on Lola's shoulder. Chandeliers give the room a warm glow, and there are thick Persian rugs on the floor. Lola embraces Constance, comforting and stroking her, a touch that gradually becomes more sexual. Because Lola knows, explains Constance, can feel through her dress why she's there.

Watching from his chair, Paw remains excluded from the main action. As Lola's servant, he is present at her grace. In this sense, his is not the typical phallic gaze. The female control and focus on the two women's pleasure is here a progressive aspect of this film, further underscored by the archaic voiceover track which runs throughout the film:

> The greedy eyes of her slave tickle across us. They stare so passionately, so deliciously; but he must wait.

As they continue to kiss, Lola begins to undress Constance, pulling her dress down her shoulders, baring her small breasts. Lola opens the bodice of her own dress as well to let Constance lick and kiss her breasts, and begins to finger Constance. A heavy rock music plasters the pictures of the two licking, kissing — naked now — while Paw still watches.

At one point, the two women approach Paw and kneel down on each side of his chair. Lola sucks him first, showing Constance how before it's her turn, after which the women return to the sofa where they continue making out. Paw follows them, caressing and kissing whatever skin he can reach, sneaking his head in between the two bodies. He masturbates until he comes. And, as opposed to the typical money shot in mainstream porn where the woman lustfully swallows the man's semen, Paw is left to

> lick off his sperm from his fingers while Constance continues to lick Lola's vulva, "earn[ing] the right to learn in Lola's house."

Whereas this first sex scene features female control and agency, the following scene casts Constance in the stereotypical role of a woman at the mercy of her unruly womanly desire for a strong man—Eg, Lola's forester and lover—to take her. In stark contrast to the scene's soft setting—Constance's bedroom with a romantic four-poster bed—the music in this scene is almost menacing, alluding to the forbidden nature of the act. And before long, she—Lola—is there: cast as the dominatrix, dressed in hardcore black shining leather and latex, with long black ribbons in her hair and thick black make-up.

> Lola promptly undresses, her flashing eyes scolding Constance who withdraws to a corner of the bed as Lola gets into it, straddling Eg, riding him as Constance watches with a longing gaze, crawling around them like an animal, kissing Eg's lips or cock when available, or Lola's skin. The experienced Lola sucks, pulls, and kisses Eg greedily. Then Eg pushes Constance away so he can penetrate Lola in traditional missionary position. Before he comes, he pulls out of her, drags off his condom, and jerks his cock a few more times until he comes, spraying his sperm on Lola's belly, depositing his male bravura, which Lola smears over her skin in line with mainstream porn.
>
> A monotonous synthesizer rhythm surrounds the shots of this scene, emphasizing the mechanical ritualistic quality of the sex. And indeed, "it's a game, a ritual,

arranged by the mistress of desire. Now she'll be bound." Eg lays Lola down on her belly and binds her arms on her back before carrying her away in his arms.

From Constance's softly lit bedroom, the film cuts to a dungeon, dark except for the dim glow of a few burning torches. Eg lays Lola down on a black blanket on top of a low bench of wooden planks on the dirt floor, "the altar of vice where anything may happen;" where "pain and pleasure strangely combine." Paw is already there, locked in a tiny cage, watching greedily, sucking his thumb.

A thumping synthesizer beat charges the shots in this scene where we see more ritualistic sex and power play. At one point, Constance, now "tested" and "forgiven," joins them in the dungeon, dressed in a black harness of leather and nails, ready to be "initiated." Joining them in the ritualistic group sex is another slave dressed in black leather, black make-up, a metal horn attached to his forehead.

An abrupt cut brings us back to Lola's salon for a surrealistic party scene celebrating Constance's initiation. Reminiscent of Knud's queer underground films, it's a full-blown kitschy campy postmodern fetish orgy, the partiers dressed in overdone drag, toasting with champagne from silver goblets, dancing in trance-like movements to a hypnotizing house music, sexually, together or alone, stripping or copulating. The filming here moves as if on speed through frantic cutting between close-ups from numerous angles spliced together.

Genders blur in this bizarre scene, the dreamy quality emphasized by handwriting from the diary floating on top of the pictures in golden letters like a dim filter. But the embellished letters are also suggestive of old-fashioned romance. "I have fallen into the dizzying well of love," writes Constance, who in the end prefers to share her four-poster with Paw with whom she has fallen in love. A slow pulsing rhythm of seventies disco enters the picture where they lie in bed. Gone is the black make-up; back is a natural looking Constance in white cotton underwear.

In crosscuts between Constance and Paw we see Lola, also "struck by loving longing," preparing to see her beloved by shaving and fingering her pussy, before chasing out into the night, draped in a black cape with a wide hood, leaving Constance and Paw to themselves in bed, in missionary position.

The moon leads way through the forest to Eg who awaits Lola in his barn-like hut, moonlight filtering down into his quarters through the hayloft above. When Lola arrives, she first assumes her position as mistress of the house, dropping her cape nonchalantly, naked beneath except for a black garter belt and stockings. She approaches Eg at the wooden tub where he is cooling down, hot from desire; she strokes his back, takes a washcloth to help him, turns him around to face her.

But then Eg shifts the power balance, holding her out in front of him before laying her down in his arms in classical Hollywood style, bending over to kiss her along her neck. This introduces the film's concluding sex scene, which moves through the typical positions. She appears to come while he's taking her in missionary, he with a money shot on her belly.

The film ends with a brief shot of Constance's great-granddaughter closing the diary as a woman begins to sing a slow bluesy song,

> When I'm alone in my house, my hand gets inside my
> blouse. After some time, after some cigarettes, and after
> some wine: you gave me something to remember, some
> place to run to. I see your memory inside of me.
>
> And while the credits scroll over the screen, a picture of Eg
> and Lola—kissing on a green hill in the woods, a faint
> sunrise in the background, he in a white cotton shirt,
> suspenders keeping his homely pants up, she in a simple
> blue cotton dress with white stripes, a shoulder bare—
> rests in the background.

I simply can't help finding it bothersome that the women in
Constance, and also as we shall see in *All About Anna*, always
want traditional monogamous love in the end, and sex in
missionary position. When the women in these two films explore
casual sex and other forms of sex before that, it is then explained
(or dismissed?!) as a part of the woman's sexual journey prior to
her arrival at her final destination of love.

Perhaps I am too strict in my judgment of these films' ultimate
recourse to stereotypical conventions about gender, sex, and
love. However, the featuring of the conventional in, say,
Candida's *The Bridal Shower*—where it serves as the starting point
for sexual exploration; where the characters expand on their
sexual repertoires; and where the gender roles evolve from the
more dichotomous to a freer floating play where initiative and
control rotate—is so much more interesting to me than the
featuring of it in *Constance* where the representation of gender
roles reverts from undermining, with Lola in charge, to patriarchal, with Eg having re-seized the control.

Applying Mulvey's critique, I see Constance playing the part
of the one who arouses desire, and the one who must be helped,

but also punished. Lola, on the other hand, is cast as the one who arouses dread, but also desire: a desire to take and to tame her unconventional authority, having seized the power from men where they have been used to holding it, triggering desire mixed with envy and anger. And so she too is punished, even if it is staged by herself. In any case, she is ultimately brought down by Eg in the film's concluding scene. When as if she's come to her senses, and struck by longing, she accedes to her need for a man.

Mulvey is also famous for the terms "gaze" and "to-be-looked-at-ness," which she introduces in the same article to expand on the female role as the object of the male gaze. Of course, Lola has her sex slaves that she might enjoy looking at when not (or while) served by, but it is still primarily the women who are looked at in this film—by the male characters, by the camera, and by the audience—even in the film's opening scene where Lola asserts and maintains her position.

Progressive power play

Lisbeth Lynghøft (b. 1962) who wrote and directed the second and most successful Puzzy Power film, *Pink Prison*, has experienced the consequences from going public about her work with porn. Like Sabina, Lisbeth had no former experience in porn; her background is in theatre as both an actor and director. On the phone with me, she talked about how she's had to work hard to prove her credibility after *Pink Prison*; about the scepticism and at times contempt she has encountered. She therefore also asked me not to blow up her name in the media. Unfortunately, this is how some of the voices of proven talent to actually make a difference and create something genuinely progressive in porn are silenced.

Lisbeth says this about how she got involved with the Puzzy Power project:

"Nothing Human is alien to me," Tennessee Williams once said. His words corresponded with my own conclusion when

I decided after several weeks of deliberation to move into a new genre and launch my own version of a porno film. In the spring of 1999, Puzzy Power, Zentropa's little sister, had been looking for female directors to advance and develop sensual porno films primarily targeted at women audiences. I met the producer, Lene Børglum, and we got on well; a few weeks later I received a phone call. "We've got a prison set—the title will be Pink Prison—we want you to write the story."

I hastily summoned all my friends—men and women— served beer and wine in the courtyard, and asked what they would like to see. It was an interesting experience, but a confusing one, too, which I may summarize by saying that everyone has his or her own favorite plot, his or her own personal desires, and more than anything else, his or her own ultimate fantasy. I listened to my friends, sought out suitable, phosphorescent cellar passages, and wrote the screenplay for Pink Prison.

In my film I very much wanted:

- To create a powerful female character who is determined and who goes with her desires.
- To write a plot that links the sex scenes and sparks off the action.
- To work on building up sensual tension between the sexes—before they have sex.
- To make the leading character into a credible figure with a life of her own and many facets to her personality.
  ...

I have no illusions that my film will revolutionize the porn industry. But I do regard it as an admirable challenge to provide my own version of what a porno film can also be, and to take part in the crossover wave—building bridges between fiction and porn.[4]

In my opinion, Pink Prison—which won a Venus Award as Best Scandinavian Film at the international adult industry trade fair VENUS in Berlin 2003—lives up to Lisbeth's goals for it. In fact, with touches of a tongue-in-cheek sense of humour that highlight the film's reflective take on porn, *Pink Prison* shatters traditional gender roles and breaks free from erotic conventions.

Filmed on the sets built for von Trier's *Dancer in the Dark* (2000), *Pink Prison* is about a thirty-two-year-old female photographer and journalist, Mila, who breaks into a notorious prison where only men are allowed in order to secure an interview with its media-shy warden Sam. Opposing not only the phallic female-objectifying gaze of mainstream porn, but also its homophobia, the film features Mila both watching men masturbating, and men having sex together as she searches through the prison for Sam. Lisbeth captures both the power and sensuality of male bodies and sexuality in these scenes.

Reflecting on what she would consider a feminist re-vision of porn, Williams concludes that, since porn has always been a male speculation on sex and female sexuality, "perhaps the true measure of the feminist re-vision of pornography would be if it were to produce a pornographic 'speculation' about the still relatively unproblematized pleasures of men."[5] Mila performs such a feminist re-vision of pornography on her journey through the prison, examining the different bodies, desires and pleasures of a range of men. At the same time she also explores her own sexual desires, defining her sexuality on her terms.

In contrast to both Constance's and Lola's ultimate dependence on men, Mila comes across as a self-assured and independent woman, in charge from beginning to end. She manoeuvres her camera with confident precision, dressed in tight jeans, a black pullover, black glasses, and her long blond hair in pigtails, one over each shoulder. "Get lost," she dismisses her editor Yasia when he tosses her a "does your work turn you on?" in the opening scene where she's shooting pictures of two women and a man, the three naked except for a few white shreds of cloth, posing behind the bars of a white cell. She signals to him to throw her a pack of cigarettes; eases one out with her long nails.

On her smoking break, putting new film in her camera, Mila makes a bet with Yasia that for her next book project she'll get into the so-called Pink Prison for an interview with its warden Sam. Yasia shakes his head at her. But in response to his doubtful response—"Let's see; how many tried that before you? Six or seven hundred? And they weren't even women"—she butts in with a "stop patronizing me. Prisons actually turn me on, a lot. There's nothing like a good long dirty captivity." The two agree that if Mila wins the bet, all the profit from the book she's now completing will go to her. If she loses, she'll spend a weekend in Paris with Yasia. In other words, it's pretty much a win-win situation for Mila who doesn't seem to mind much the idea of a trip to Paris; the flirting goes both ways.

And this is where the film's score sets in with more momentum, a catchy rhythm with lyrics by Lisbeth sung by a husky woman's voice, setting the tone for the film:

When you want to break out, I'm the one who breaks in. I'm obsessed with the delicate methods of sin. Don't expect I'll beat you. There's a spite in my vein. A prisoner of lust and a sucker for pain, I'm your captive by choice.

The music bleeds into the next scene featuring Mila on her way to the prison.

Unable to convince the gatekeeper to let her in, Mila manages to break in to the prison through an air vent at night. An apprehensive drumming underscores the charged tension of Mila crawling through the dark narrow duct, in the background the sounds of gates slamming. Then she sees a man, standing with his back towards her. The light is dimmed, the walls within the prison a deep red hue. She turns off her flashlight and studies him.

The camera shifts to study him from the front, framing his body. He is holding on to the rods of the gate to his cell. In the background behind him we see a sink to the left; the air vent down to the right, just above the floor. The contours of Mila's head are vaguely visible behind the screen, the pale shimmer from her face and hair. The man removes his shirt, turns around to put it on his cot, and, with his body facing Mila, begins to stroke his chest with his hands, over his abdomen, down into his pants, touching himself, moaning. The camera crosscuts continuously between studying him and Mila watching him; she gasps with anticipation.

The sound of more intense moaning draws her in its direction; she casts a lingering gaze at the half-naked man still touching himself, his eyes closed, before crawling on. The synthesizer music swells, the beat quicker. In the next cell, she finds two men engaged in raw passionate sex. Mila unbuttons the top buttons of her shirt, slips a hand in beneath it, and begins to touch her breasts. She lets go of a sigh and one of the men turns around in her direction. She quickly withdraws while the camera lingers on the two men.

Stylistically, the film well captures the charged excitement of Mila's search for Sam. The camerawork builds tension through crosscuts between Mila watching and what she sees, undisclosed. The unnerving echoes of gates and locks being opened or shut in the background, at times the menacing sound of a dog barking, hard steps of boots over concrete, occasionally the faint sound of a siren, all add further atmosphere. The editing is seamless.

Mila's journey through the prison features her not just watching others have sex, however, but also her taking part in it, playing both the part of the one in charge and the one at the mercy. The sex scenes range from muted intimacy to lustful desire, soulful passion, power-and-domination role-play, and a bit of rough sex, all accompanied by well-composed matching soundtracks.

One of my favorite scenes is the kitchen scene where Mila has sex with the chef among a buffet of colorful dishes (prepared as a midnight snack for Sam), which they playfully include in their steamy sex. Accompanied by a lively rhythm, this scene portrays a richly visual and sensual feast à la *Nine ½ Weeks*, but without the manipulative power play of the character performed there by Mickey Rourke. A gender equal rotation of initiative, and a democratic positioning of their bodies instead characterize the sexual encounter between Mila and the chef. And whereas the chemistry between the characters of Rourke and Kim Basinger becomes sickly ultra-tense, the atmosphere here remains completely relaxed. The two are simply having a really good time together; she giggly, and he with a warm big grin on his face throughout.

A soft rhythm introduces their encounter and their sensual kisses, licks, and caresses as the two mutually touch and explore each other's bodies. She gets up onto a countertop; opens her legs to him. He takes her foot, kisses and licks it, then her leg, all the way down to her pussy where he lingers; licking and fingering her.

Then he lifts her up and carries her to the buffet table where he sets her down among all the food, and this is where the kitchen party really takes off to the sound of a vivacious beat. Mila begins: dipping a strawberry in cream and shoving it into this mouth. Another one, the stem still on; he tries to spit it out, she giggles, he laughs. They kiss. He takes a handful of strawberries and crushes them in his hand before letting the juice and flesh of the berries gush over her breasts for him to gobble up. She takes another handful of strawberries, herself crushing them; liquid and mush slide down her arm as she feeds him with it. "Yay, cook for me baby," he laughs, licking her arm. On to the watermelon, tomatoes; juices flowing, both of them licking, guzzling, devouring. He picks up a long cucumber, laughs at her. She gives it a fake blowjob, takes a crunching bite of it; he laughs jollily. She moves it down towards her pussy where he takes over, tickling her with it. Then on to a half peeled banana, slithering it down her back, between her buttocks, towards her pussy. Thirsty, he swigs the champagne in large gulps from the bottle. She pours herself an overflowing glass.

Mila dips her hand in a bowl of cream before stroking his penis with her cream dripping fingers, and then sucking his cream covered penis. She lies down on her back on top of the table and the camera captures her pussy in close-up; her clitoris protrudes from the head of her swollen labia. Standing by the edge of the table, the chef pulls on a condom; she adjusts to allow him inside, folding her legs around his hips. The camera frames their glistening bodies, their hips and bodies rocking, intertwined. Spliced in between are close-ups of his penis hugged in and out by her vagina. At the moment she appears to come, her hand knocks a milk bottle over; the camera zooms in on the milk pouring out. An allusion to the money shot, but here, in a twist; that of a woman's. He comes while still inside of her, his face contracting in pleasure. They linger in their embrace.

* * *

As we find out in the film's concluding scene, the prison warden Sam is in fact a woman—Samantha—a dominatrix with an appetite for power play. Having secured Sam's liking, Mila finally obtains the interview she set out to get, topping off her prison adventure.

Leaving the prison, she finds Yasia curled up in the corner of an open jeep, wet from the rain, his clothes rumpled. She throws him the tape from the voice recorder.

"No Paris?" he asks.

"Who knows, maybe," she retorts teasingly. She looks fresh and well rested in jeans and a black pullover, her glasses back on, completely on top of things.

"Come on, let's go," she continues as she grabs the cigarette he just lit from his mouth and places it between her own lips while reaching for the keys; "I'll drive." With a grin that says this is so typical Mila, he hands them over to her.

In the film's final shot, Mila with Yasia onboard drives

> away from the prison, not into the sunset, nor the sunrise, but down a wet road on a rather gray morning while the credits scroll over the screen, accompanied by the song from the film's opening scene: "Captive by choice."

In agreement with contemporary gender equality politics, *Pink Prison* portrays a rotation of power between the opposite genders. The film's meditation on control is interesting not just for its emphasis on gender equality, however. *Pink Prison* features both women and men getting a kick both from being in control and *surrendering* control. As modern beings in a competitive society where it seems imperative that we constantly remain on top of things, sexual abandon may appear an appealing pause from the daily pressure to always measure up in a culture that gauges success according to accomplishments. Perhaps in light of the conflicting demands modern women in particular seem to face—to do it all, both what a man can do and also "what a woman does"—women feel this pressure even more so than men.

Despite the gender progressive aspects of *Pink Prison*, and also partly *Constance*, Zentropa's Puzzy Power production caused several of the company's investors to withdraw their financial support. Zentropa therefore delegated the handling of Puzzy Power to Innocent Pictures, run by porn reviewer Nicolas Barbano and porn producer for television Claus Sørensen. Lene had also struggled to find international distributors for the films, in particular in the United States. As she told me, her extensive international network and experience in making international deals for von Trier did little in helping her do business with major porno moguls. And the harder it got, the creepier the entire business seemed to her. And when her son started school, she wanted to protect him from any potential mockery too.

Heart Core romance

As it turned out, Innocent Pictures also encountered challenges working with major porn investors and distributors in conjunction with the production of their first—and so far only— Puzzy Power film, *All About Anna* (2005). In particular because the director Jessica Nilsson (b. 1965) and leading actress Gry Bay (b. 1974) wanted a less explicit film while the film's producer, Nicolas Barbano (b. 1963), had financed and contracted the film as a hardcore film. On the film's extra material, Jessica, a graduate of the Danish Film School with an indie, alternative approach to filmmaking, makes it clear that she is critical to porn, but that she agreed to take part in this film's making because it was supposed to be different from mainstream porn. Speaking with me on the phone, Jessica expressed frustration with the making of the film, in particular the external involvement. In the end, Jessica left the project before the film was completed because of disagreements with the producers. The DVD does include Jessica's unedited version, which has a quirkier slapstick take on the story that might have rescued the film from its final portentousness. On the other hand, it might just reflect Jessica's mixed feelings about porn that could have interfered with a truthful approach to the characters and their desires.

Described by the producer as an erotic "Heart Core Feature," *All About Anna* is a softer Puzzy Power film. Focusing on the theme of love and relationships, the film successfully incorporates the sex in a seamless manner; however, the predominant sex featured is conventional: women are taken either in missionary position or from behind. Only the vulgar drunk roommate of the main character is seen riding her lover. Overall, the film further rehashes the gender stereotypes we saw in *Constance*, introduced in the film's two-minute long trailer:

A young woman ... in search of herself

The adventurer ... will he break her heart ... again?
A French actress ... the first to understand
The seductress ... from whom no-one is safe...

Anna is a young costume designer who in the opening scene is captured in romantic bliss onboard a Greenlandic icebreaker together with her beau Johan, a blond muscular Viking, three-day beard and his hair ruffled. Shot as a flashback in slow motion to the sounds of a guitar playing, we see the two fishing, kissing, laughing. Johan is an adventurous vagabond, explains Anna in voiceover, who has since taken off for the North Pole. He was supposed to be gone for three months, but the letters stopped coming after only a couple of months. Five years later she still hasn't heard anything. Now she looks at herself in the mirror and wipes away her tears and streaks of black mascara. She determines that enough is enough, touches up her make-up, and lets her blond hair down. The sound-track shifts to noisy hard rock, and dressed in black, Anna marches down the stairs of her apartment building, heading out into the night, out on the town. From now on life is going to be all about fun, she declares, she will party and have sex and she will no longer make herself emotionally vulnerable to anyone.

But of course it doesn't look like she's having much fun at all, though we at times hear her giggling, mostly because she's drunk. Flashbacks of Johan continue to haunt her. She gets smashed in bars, has sex on public toilets and in alleys, needing help to get home, for instance by the softhearted dull Frank with whom she enters a half-hearted relationship. On clear autumn days we see her looking longingly at other women strolling their children while moving trucks pass her, and we sense that deep inside she dreams about a husband and children within the comfort of a home.

In the end Anna gets her Johan back, having realized first that she needs to break the cycle; she has to be willing to let herself be vulnerable again, towards Johan. If she keeps seeking comfort in strangers, she'll end up lonely and bitter. Johan, on the other hand, comes to the realization that "maybe fun's not enough anymore." The film concludes with Anna reunited with Johan, the two having barely escaped losing one another yet again because of some mutual misunderstandings. In the final scene we see them making love on the icebreaker. A win-win situation for Johan, in other words, while Anna gets what she apparently needs to be happy: a real man.

Anna is a modern version of Constance, a young woman with long blond locks and big blue eyes in need of help to understand what she needs. She receives this first from the French bisexual theater actress Sophie. Anna gets to know Sophie in Paris where she's been offered a gig at a theater as the talented costume designer she presumably is. Sophie offers her friendship and comfort, including a sexual type of "sweet caress" where she strokes, kisses, licks, and gently fingers Anna until she comes. Sophie's sad side—an unresolved love affair—makes Anna see that she needs to give her relationship with Johan another chance. Anna also learns this lesson from her roommate Camilla ("the seductress") with whom she shares an apartment in Copenhagen. Cast as a wanton vulgar woman with long black hair and dark make-up, Camilla represents that which Anna does not want to become. Camilla is, among other things, guilty of hitting on Johan when he returns to Denmark in search of his beloved. Truth be told, Camilla doesn't know that this Johan is 'Anna's Johan' (and Anna is at this point in Paris), and 'poor' Johan does do his best to protect himself from her, but the thing is, of course, that 'he's just a guy' and so he can't really help himself when she pulls out all her tricks on him to seduce and satisfy him with a blowjob. In the end even Frank helps Anna realize that she has to find the courage to give love a chance. Before a "good night" and "good luck" on a night she comes to him for comfort, well after having dumped him in the first place, he insists that she must find Johan and tell him what he means to her, "or you'll spend the rest of your life thinking love hurts."

As I see it then, *All About Anna* provides another illustration of Mulvey's model of the woman as the object of desire (Anna) or fear (Camilla) who must be either helped (Anna) or punished (Camilla, but after she's been rejected and chastised, even cried her big tears, she too comes to see that love is what matters, and then in the end even she gets her beloved Albert).

Yet, despite the film's stereotypical portrayal of gender, sex, and love, *All About Anna* has become a huge success among audiences, and not just in Denmark. The DVD hit double platinum in Scandinavia and also in Germany where it was contracted for adult television and has played frequently on the satellite television channel Beate-Uhse.TV. In the United States, where the film is distributed by Wicked Pictures, the film was nominated for four awards, including for best foreign feature, at the Adult Video News Awards (AVN), also known as the Oscar ceremony for porn.[6] In fact, all Puzzy Power films have sold extremely well.[7] I imagine the films' motion picture format and connections to a well-established film production company are reassuring to an audience for whom porn is new and perhaps a little intimidating while at the same time enticing. And this is in itself a good thing: attracting an audience that might otherwise have remained in the dark about the potential of new porn.

* * *

After losing a court case in September 2010 against the amusement park company Tivoli A/S for using the word "Tivoli" in the title for its erotic entertainment series "Tivoli Night," Innocent Pictures was eventually forced to claim bankruptcy in November 2011. Zentropa—which still owns Puzzy Power—has resumed the handling and distributing of all the Puzzy Power films. Reflecting a cultural climate that is becoming ever more open towards progressive explicit sex films, von Trier recently announced that in 2012 he intends to make a sexually explicit film, which will follow the erotic life of a woman from infancy to middle age. A softcore version for television and mainstream cinema will also be made.[8]

Perhaps von Trier's announcement is also a sign that Zentropa will yet again attempt to create progressive quality porn that appeals to women. And that would be a welcome development on behalf of a reputable film production company, signaling support for the significance of new re-visioned, gender democratic porn.

Chapter 3

Easy on the Eye: Britain's First Female Porn Director

British humor in Anna Span's porn for women and men
British Anna Span (b. 1972) represents a new generation of porn
re-visionists. After working for the British porn channel
Television X in editing, cutting scenes to avoid British censorship;
and also in production, shooting a show about two girlfriends,
art students and strippers on the side, she founded her own Easy
on the Eye Productions company and launched a line of porn
under the banner "Genuine Female Point of View – From Britain's
First Female Director."

Great Britain has a long history in censoring "indecent" or
"obscene" images. In response to the arrival of video porn, the R-
18 certificate was introduced in the early 80s, requiring all video
films be subject to the classification procedures of the British
Board of Film Certification (BBFC). The sale of films rated R-18
was restricted to a limited amount of licensed sex shops while
softcore films rated 18—largely devoid of sex—could be sold in
general shops where children were allowed too. With the R-18
rated videos censored to comply with strictly interpreted laws,
there was, however, very little difference between the 18 and R-
18 rated versions.

In response to a growing black market and a lowering of
customs barriers after the UK joined the European Union, the
BBFC in 2000 decided to liberalize its R-18 porn video classification to allow explicit hardcore scenes. Films rated R-18 are still
only allowed as merchandise in stores with special license, and
not via mail order or from the Internet. Anna started to sell her
films through the female-run sex shop Ann Summers and other
sex shops licensed to sell R-18 rated DVDs. She also found

vendors in other countries. Because most of the economic profit is in distribution and direct sale, and because Video on Demand (VOD) escapes the laws that pertain to DVDs, Anna eventually also set up her own online shop at her site where she sells VOD clips from her DVDs. Her films are also available as VOD clips from other companies' sites, including from the San Francisco-based online adult store GameLink.

Like Candida, Anna is well educated and presents a critical approach to her work. She has a Bachelor's in Film and Video from Central St. Martin's School of Art, a reputable art and design school in the center of London. She also has a Master's in Philosophy from Birkbeck College and is currently studying for a Ph.D. in Gender Studies at Sussex University. Her thesis from St. Martin's, *Towards a New Pornography*, discusses what a female perspective in porn would look like and also filmically; what makes an image sexy. Anna makes it clear in her thesis that she considers pornography an underdeveloped and under-investigated area in film.

Originally Anna was, however, an anti-porn feminist who considered porn discriminating and exploitative of women. But then at one point it struck her that the real problem was that porn has been made to satisfy men, not women. As she explains it on her website:

Originally, Anna was anti-porn, believing it to be an area in which men were given free reign to subjugate the woman for their own needs. This was the late 80's in the height of the "ban the top shelf" campaign led by Clare Short in the UK. But then she had "a moment of truth" walking down Old Compton Street in the red light district of Soho, London. She deconstructed her feeling of anger, asked herself why she felt this way and the honest answer was she was jealous. She was jealous that men had their Soho. The society that we lived in said that a man's desires were worth investing money in to cater for. She felt that what was missing was the equivalent (but very different in content/style) for women. Why shouldn't a woman have the subconscious confidence that even if she doesn't personally want to use porn, she knows that the world in which she lives, recognises that she might want to and recognises her right to do so.[1]

Anna's porn reflects a new generation's more relaxed approach to both sex and porn. While Candida shows a concern for sexual hang-ups and how to overcome these, including insecurities about the use of porn, the attitude to sex and porn in Anna's porn is easygoing and playful. Psychological complexes or guilty feelings don't trouble the characters in Anna's porn. Shame about sex is only referred to as something comical, by for instance the patient Mark in "Supply Nurse" on *A & O Department* (2004; A & O—Anal & Oral—is a wordplay on A & E, short for Accident & Emergency, the British version of the ER) when he stutters "but I'm a Christian!" to the female nurse's suggestion he masturbates to get his hard-on down, an erection she (purposefully) caused by "mistreating" him with Viagra. Women and men in Anna's porn pretty much have an uncomplicated relationship to sex, even casual sex. Even Mark gleefully surrenders to some sex with the nurse—who turns out not to be a nurse but a lusty lady in borrowed uniform—under the pretext of treating his erection.

While Candida's films portray a range of sexual encounters, from the most tender to the more passionate, all the sex in Anna's porn is quite steamy. And whereas Candida avoids lingering on close-ups of genitalia and usually steers clear of the money shot, there are plenty of both in Anna's porn. Anna also shows anal penetration, which is only alluded to in Candida's films.

Candida is concerned that sex scenes between girls may seem gratuitous; an ingredient added to please a male audience. Anna is not so worried about that. In her world sex between girls is a natural part of everyday life and not just between lesbian and bisexual women. Sex between girls is something that easily can take place between girlfriends and colleagues, say if they've had a little bit too much to drink.

Group sex is also common in Anna's porn, but in contrast to the group sex in mainstream porn, there is often a majority of men for the women to savor and be double penetrated by in Anna's group sex scenes. The female initiative and control are in any case key characteristics of all the group sex episodes, whether the women are in the majority or not. The DVD *Be My Toy Boy* (2009) focuses primarily on MILF: sex between mature women and young men. MILF, short for "moms I'd like to fuck," was popularized by the horny high school boys in *American Pie* (1999), but for the mothers on this DVD it would be more accurate to speak about "the young men we moms would like to fuck."

Anna has won many fans for her sense of humor. In fact, Anna uses humor as a tool in her porn more than any of the other filmmakers I've looked at. And not along the crass lines done in mainstream porn.[2] Anna uses humor to capture chemistry between characters as they teasingly flirt and fool around. She also develops hilarious scenarios in the British tradition of Benny Hill. The episode "Sperm Sample" on *A & O Department* relies on both kinds of humor. In typical Anna style it also shows a lot of steamy sex, with the woman in charge. For in Anna's porn, women often take the initiative and they will not let the sex be over until they are satisfied. Their actual orgasms are also convincingly captured: the hectic flushing spreading around the neck as they approach, the shivering quivers over face and body when they come.

In the opening scene we see a female doctor busy in her lab, with glass bottles, jars, and funnels on the shelves, cylinders and more equipment on her workbench. A janitor enters the room; he's there to mop the floor. They are both attractive; she with dark hair in a pony tale, white coat, and high heels (!); he in blue coat, blond ruffled hair, a boyish look in his face. She's studying something in a microscope, taking notes. He looks at her, curiously, while mopping.

"So what's that you're doing there?"
    "Oh, just some research."
    "So what is it you're researching?"
    "Stem cells."
    "What are they then?"
    She looks up from her work, exasperated: "Stem cells."
    He stops to mop, a smile lurking on his lips;
    "Did you know I'm training to be a doctor?"
    "Really?"
    "Don't you believe me? I sit my exams next week."
    "Well, really, no to be quite honest, because if, if you were training to be a doctor you wouldn't be a hospital porter, would you?"
    "But you gotta start somewhere."
    "Yes, that's why we all start in medical school, not by being a porter."
    "I'm taking a different road."
    "Obviously."

He goes on with a series of teasingly naïve questions; she retorts, somewhat exasperated, but not unfazed by the playful tone. He pauses to give her a break, leans up against a bench, unbuttons his coat. She looks in his direction. At the lump in his pants. She adjusts her glasses:

"I'm not being funny, but have you had that checked out?"
   "What, what's wrong with it?"
   "Well, it looks rather inflamed. I think you may have elephantitis of the penis."
   "No, you don't think so."
   "Uhum."
   "Where should I go and get it checked out then?"
   "Obviously: your doctor."
   "You're a doctor."
   "Oh, so you're trying to say you want me to check it out for you."
   "Well you noticed it."

She sighs, faking annoyance.

"Ok, get it out and let me have a look."
   "Looks all right to me," he says feeling his crotch.
   "Oh, get it out," she snaps impatiently;
   "There's nothing wrong with it!" he insists.
   "Come here," she brushes him off, "so I can have a look."

He walks towards her.

"Not too close!"

He unzips his pants to get it out.

"Oh, it's obviously too big, you can't get it out of your pants," she remarks flippantly; "Yes, yes; a definite case of elephantitis. Do you have trouble fitting that inside your girlfriend?"

"Well, now that you come to mention it; yeah."

"Hmm, I better try it out. Lie down; come on! I'll take a closer look."

"Should I take this off?"

"Yes! Take your trousers off!"

She puts a towel on an examination table, has him lie down on top of it. Studies his penis closely.

"When you're excited, does this get any bigger?" she asks, straight-faced.

"Well, yes, it does, actually."

"I definitely need to see how big it gets."

She begins to jerk his cock.

"I'm going to have to see if this fits in my mouth; is that okay?"

"Yeah."

In this manner the playful and eventually quite bustling breathless sex continues as she proceeds to deep throat him too and then decides to see if she can fit his penis in her vagina, and anus, from the front and behind, and so on and on. She gets sweaty and flushed from all the work, as does he. She comes before him as he takes her from behind anally while she stimulates herself with her fingers. At the end she requests a sperm sample. She puts on gloves, finds a sterile reagent bottle; holds it up to the head of his penis and has him masturbate until he comes. It's a hilarious

> scenario, and of course sperm ends up spraying all over the place rather than into the narrow bottle. Yet, straight-faced still, even as streaks of sperm are running down her face, she comments dryly as she seals the bottle: that will be it, now it must be studied in the lab, he may leave.

The episode "Head to Toe Service" on *Good Service* (2003) brings us more absurd humor. A young woman arrives in a beauty salon to have her hair done and her legs, underarms and bikini line shaved before a wedding. The male beautician has a packed schedule but offers to take care of the shaving while she's also getting her hair done. She agrees without hesitation despite the presence of other customers around her. She slips off her clothes, and gets comfortable in the chair with a magazine. And when the beautician asks if she would like him to lick away a little nick he unfortunately caused while shaving her bikini line, she thanks him with a yes and thus also receives a good dose of cunnilingus and fingering to top off her treatment. Which in turn results in steamy sex.

Powerful pussy pictures

In her use of close-ups of genitalia, Anna's porn resembles mainstream porn more so than Candida's films do. However, there is a difference in the close-ups of genitalia in Anna's porn versus those in mainstream porn. In style, Anna's pussy pictures come closer to those of feminist artist and female masturbation activist Betty Dodson (b. 1929). Dodson has made a series of DVDs, including *Self-Loving: Portrait of a Woman's Sexuality Seminar* (1991), *Celebrating Orgasm: Women's Private Selfloving Sessions* (1997), and *Viva la Vulva: Women's Sex Organs Revealed* (1998), which feature women getting together to learn about and admire their own vulva and those of other women, and the pleasurable sensations these are capable of arriving at with different kinds of stimulation. The pictures of pussies in Dodson's film emphasize their natural beauty, as do the pussy pictures in Anna's porn. Anna's pussy pictures are juicy and sexy, capturing the layered textures and richly hued luster of the vulvae. And like for instance Dodson's *Viva la Vulva*—which presents us with Dodson and ten other naked women of different body type, skin color, and age, ranging from twenty-five to sixty-eight, all posing for their pussy portraits—Anna's porn too captures an amazing multitude of *different* kinds of pussies, even if in a different context. There are vulvae in a variety of different shapes, colors, and sizes, including of the outer and inner labia, and of the clitorises, some covered, others protruding. And we get to see how vulvae change in tune with arousal and pleasure, labia swelling, their colors deeper, the sheen wetter.

But it's not just the power and beauty of pussies that make Anna's pictures of them good. The quality of the pictures, which are shot digitally, is also a factor. Overall, Anna shows that she too has a good eye for picture composition, from the particular details to the framed setting.

In for example "Holloway Rd. Market" on *Pound a Punnet* (2003), the location and setting of each shot becomes important for the atmosphere of the sexual encounter. All the episodes on this DVD are shot gonzo-style with Anna involved in the action.

In this particular episode, Anna is having lunch with her girlfriends Amber and Jo, lounging outside on the roof deck of an old red brick apartment building one of those early warm spring days.

As the audience we're pulled right into the action from the opening scene where Anna and Amber are walking, chatting, on their way to Jo who's selling fish at one of

---

London's busy markets. It's her lunch break soon, and after a little bantering with her colleague, they all head home to Jo's. Their lunch is simple: store bought sandwiches wrapped in plastic and orange juice. What the girls really are enjoying is the fact that spring is here and that it's warm enough to eat outside, though it's still early in the season; many of the trees and shrubs around them are still brown without leaves.

Those who live in colder winter climates can relate to the girls' giddy desire to absorb every little warm sunray during their brief lunch break. We hear traffic in the distance, otherwise just the girls chitchatting, glasses clinking on the trey, the plastic being pulled off the sandwiches. If a bird had chirped or one of the cats lounging by them purred, we would have heard it. Welcome spring sounds like that give the scene a cozy warm atmosphere. This is significant, because as opposed to Candida's investment in musical soundtracks, Anna does not add additional sound to her porn, aside from the sighing and moaning. (On her first DVD—*Anna's Mates*, 2004—Anna did add some synthesizer pop music to a couple of the episodes. Sometimes it works, other times it's just disturbing, especially since it's sometimes a bit of a challenge to catch what the characters in Anna's porn are saying, both because of their British accent, but also because of the technology Anna uses with no additional microphones).

Lounging in the sun the girls get warm; Jo takes off her jeans and Amber unbuttons her dress. She's not wearing a bra and wonders if perhaps she might borrow a bikini from Jo? The lazy spring giddiness continues in Jo's sunny bedroom where they rummage through drawers for a bikini while bantering, teasing and admiring each other's bodies.

A celebration of bodies in different shapes and sizes thus becomes a central point in this episode. Jo is tall and thin while Amber is shorter and plumper. Jo makes the first comment, about how luscious Amber is, her bum and boobs; if she could just feel them a little? Their little flirt is distinguished by its quiet humor and warmth, but all the mutual adoration and exhibition of bodies excite the girls and in the end they are giddily engaged in sex while Anna continues filming.

If it hadn't been for the fact that the girlfriends behave in a manner that's so natural and trusting—while also playful and bubbly—I might have dismissed the episode between Jo and Amber as a "gratuitous" girl-girl sex scene. But it reminds me less of a typical porn cliché and more of what recent research has found about how women appear to be far more open to same-sex encounters than men. In a recent survey, more than twice as many females as males reported some type of sexual encounter with a member of the same sex at some point in their lifetime, providing empirical support for the popular assumption that women have more fluidity in their sexual attraction than do men.[3] I don't get the impression that this is something the two girls have a habit of doing, at least not Amber. Jo is more forward, and they are at her house, and then: "Why not," Amber might think. "Why not try this? And see if it feels good." To feel another woman's body next to hers, similar, because they're both girls, but also different.

Sex manuals and sexological films by a new generation of bold feminist sex educators, including in the US by Tristan Taormino and Jamye Waxman (whose work I shall return to in my next chapter), instruct today's audiences on same sex among women, sex with sex toys, strap-on sex, anal sex, group sex, and BDSM. Anna avoids BDSM, because that would have made her porn illegal for sale in Great Britain, but there is quite a bit of girl-girl sex, use of sex toys, anal sex, and group sex. It's usually not clear if the girls who're having sex are hetero, bisexual or lesbian; they're just having sex together. In some episodes it appears that the girl-girl sex is a result of sexual exploration, or inebriation.

In for instance "Columbia Road Market, London, E2," another episode on *Pound a Punnet*, the bride-to-be Vicky has sex with her lesbian flower arranger Taylor. Vicky is afraid she'll otherwise miss out on something untried before she gets married, and Taylor gladly and graciously steers Vicky through her first same-sex sexual encounter. In "The Cut, Waterloo, London SE1," also on *Pound a Punnet*, two women are inspired to some intimate play when reminded of how they used to do so as children after one of them receives new underwear as a gift from her mom. The study mates Elizabeth and Avalon in "Shoot the Slut" on *Play the Slut* (2004) want to portray the sexual side of women for a video project they're working on for a feminist film studies seminar, and therefore film their mutual stimulation with various sex toys.

In "China Chelsea" on *Anna's Mates*, alcohol gets the blame when the sleepless exhausted ceramic artist Angie loses all inhibitions after a few glasses of red wine at a pub close to her shop. She has just finished and sent off a big order, and relieved to be finished, she has taken a break with her younger assistant Chelsea and Anna (Span) who've offered to help clean up. Back in the workshop, Angie admits to feeling a bit "tipsy." When she helps Chelsea (who has just told them about a date she's made with a bloke she met on the train) put on an apron, she teases her first by squeezing her around the waist before pinching her tits. And then, after a slurry "You've been such a great help these last few days, I don't know what I would have done without you," she continues to hug and kiss her, and one thing leads to the other, because a giggly Chelsea is not opposed to a little girl-girl sex either.

A "female point of view:" in defense of scopophilia and voyeurism

Anna markets her porn as made from a "Genuine Female Point of View." Beyond focusing on modern self-confident women in charge of their sexuality, this also has to do with how the camera captures the characters. In an email to me, Anna explains it this way:

> Usually TV and film shoot a three way set up for a man and a woman talking to each other — one camera objective, one his POV and one her POV. This is what we are used to seeing, so it looks normal. In porn, however, her POV is usually completely removed. All I do is put it back in, as often as you would see it in a mainstream movie, say one in three shots or so. Any image mainly looking at the man in my films, I call female POV, it's not just the direct eyeline shots [from the female character's point of view]. Because I put them back in, the films resemble the usual stuff we see on TV and film.[4]

In the porn Anna shoots gonzo-style, *her* specific gaze or perspective is additionally evident as she follows and talks with the characters while she looks at and films them.

Anna's use of gonzo also highlights the scopophilic joy in watching, in fact legitimizing voyeurism; being turned on by looking at others have sex. "Neil Down for Jo" on *Anna's Mates*, for instance, features the pleasure of both Neil and Jo having sex, and also the delight of their friends Anna and Abby who watch them — Anna through her camera.

In the opening scene, Anna, Abby, and Neil are at a café, making plans to go out that night. Neil doesn't think Jo will want to join them; after she started working nights, she's always so tired. Anna insists Neil tries a little harder to get Jo to join them. If she's been so tired lately, then maybe a little "massaging and shagging" can be just the thing she needs to get into the mood. Do it, the two giggly girlfriends goad him on. And we can come with and watch you!

Jo is doing the dishes when the three arrive; she's rushed, in a hurry to get off to work. They tell her about their plans for the night, maybe she could get someone else to take her shift? After some back and forth discussion, Jo finally agrees on the condition that Neil finds someone to step in for her. Anna and Abby leave under the pretext of buying beer so they can have some drinks at Neil and Jo's before they go out, but instead they remain in the stairway from where they can watch the two above without being seen.

Typically the characters who have sex in Anna's gonzo porn know they're being watched and filmed; in other words, there's an unspoken mutual agreement among everyone involved that it's okay. Jo, on the other hand, is unaware that she and Neil are being watched. Yet, the voyeur scene in this film doesn't feel exploitative. Neil seems like a likable fellow, not like someone who would expose his girlfriend to something she wouldn't appreciate. Anna and Abby are good friends of theirs. The effect of this cordial arrangement is that the audience also gets the sense that it's okay for us to watch Neil and Jo too, together with Anna and Abby.

Like Candida's *Eyes of Desire* where Lisa uses a telescope to look at others, herself being watched too, and *The Bridal Shower* where both stripping and watching striptease and porn are discussed and defended, Anna's gonzo porn in this way stresses how both posing and having sex for the camera, as well as watching people pose and have sex, perhaps via a camera, can be positive activities. That watching another, admiring and praising his or her various attributes, the way Amber and Jo do, can be an affirming gesture and not a discriminating objectification that reduces the person to his or her parts, boobs or bums. As Anna maintains at her website:

> She believes that to sexually objectify, that is to fleetingly view a person's sexual attractiveness separately from their personality/person, is a natural human experience, NOT just a male one, as traditionally depicted.[5]

I think Anna's emphasis here on the fleeting gaze—rather than thinking of objectification as a discriminating fixation on body parts—is interesting.

Fighting the law from the outside and in

Anna's defense for sexual objectification does not however imply an uncritical attitude to the media's sexualization of women. On the contrary, Anna works against unrealistic images of idealized women in porn as well as in popular media and advertisements. Writes Anna:

> Women are bombarded with imagery in popular culture that objectifies women in order to sell us goods and services. Sexualised imagery is used in conjunction with normal, everyday items like glasses, mineral water and breakfast cereal. This is a dishonest representation of women's experience of sex and is fundamentally wrong. By accepting these images we are giving our permission to advertisers to use women's bodies as nothing more than a tool to bring them financial gain. I believe advertising should represent women fairly and not feed on insecurities of body image and self-esteem.[6]

Under her married name, Arrowsmith, Anna was the Liberal Democrats' candidate for Gravesham in Kent for the 2010 general election. Though Anna lost the election, the Liberal Democrats' vote share did see a noticeable increase. Among the political issues Anna fought for in her campaign were: mandatory comprehensive human sexuality education that covers wide ground and starts early, labeling of airbrushed pictures to build awareness of distorted images, and age limit on web pages with adult content. In her capacity as Chair of the Adult Industry Trade Association, Anna has overseen the industry's work with the relevant authorities to try to prevent underage access to pornography online.[7]

When I first met Anna in the spring of 2006, she was still in the start-up stage of her career, her office a small rented apartment above a shop in a little market street in London. Like the Puzzy Power producers Lene Børglum and Nicolas Barbano she talked to me about how difficult she's found it to penetrate the industry and find distributors when you're an independent producer of new alternative porn competing with huge porno moguls. And she talked about the resistance she's faced in general while pursuing her work, even at Central St. Martin's School of Art when she was working on her project on porn there in the late 90s.

A member of Feminists Against Censorship, which a group of feminist academics and activists founded in 1989, Anna has been an advocate for feminist porn since she started making her own porn. She has pushed for regular health screenings for people in the industry, including free testing for STIs and HIV, already granted to others whose work exposes them to physical contact, such as boxers. And she has fought the British law's prohibition of porn featuring female ejaculation, which it defines as urination and therefore obscene to portray according to the British Obscene Publications Act (OPA). In 2007, she was presented with the award for Indie Porn Pioneer at the second annual Feminist Porn Awards.

Anna told me when I first met her that she intended to test the

British law against showing female ejaculation with her DVD *Women Love Porn,* which she had just completed. After three years, the film—which includes a scene featuring a woman ejaculating—finally came out. On initial submission to the BBFC, the board requested edits to remove the female ejaculation section. Anna recruited support from among others Deborah Sundahl— an internationally known American expert on female ejaculation—and presented the BBFC with biological evidence in support of the actress' ability to ejaculate. Initially the BBFC still refused to pass the film but when Anna pushed for a hearing with the Video Appeals Committee, they retreated. Anna has claimed this as a landmark victory that sets precedence for future cases.[8] BBFC, on the other hand, has said that the amount of "urolagnia" in this film was not sufficiently significant to ensure a successful prosecution under OPA; BBFC therefore maintains that their position remains unchanged.[9] Anna has already made it clear that she is prepared to contest BBFC on this. Argues Anna: "It remains the case that <u>any</u> urolagnia falls foul of the OPA, so the passing of this and subsequent films containing female ejaculation, represent a significant change in policy by the BBFC."[10]

Women Love Porn premiered at VENUS in Berlin October 2009. Produced by Anna, the DVD contains episodes written and directed by five other women, top runners in a competition Anna arranged to encourage other women to make new porn. The winner of the competition then got the opportunity to write and direct an entire DVD with Anna as the producer. The result is Katie Coxxx's *Apocalypse Angels* (2009), the second release in Anna's "Women Love Porn" series, which now also includes *Rock Hard* (2009), written and directed by Jelena Lakic, and *Morning Glory* (2010), also by Lakic as producer and director with Anna as executive producer.

Anna has also written a handbook on how to make your own erotic home videos (*Erotic Home Video: Create Your Own Adult Films,* 2003), which came out in paperback in 2006 with a new title: *Shoot Your Own Erotic Adult Home Movies.*

Today, Anna and her husband Tim Arrowsmith live in Kent from where she runs Easy on The Eye Productions. Anna remains active in public debates and is frequently featured in the media. Most recently, she was invited by the University of Cambridge Students' Union to debate against the aforementioned Gail Dines and Shelley Lubben. The Union's proposed motion—"This house believes that pornography does a good public service"[11]—passed, but not without controversy.[12] The debate received much attention in the media, including on BBC radio.[13]

Chapter 4

New Progressive Porn: Pushing the Limits

Though the United States was the haven for porn's "golden age" and is still home to the world's largest porn production, there is far from a free float of porn here. On the contrary, the regulation of porn is strict, and attitudes towards it divided, ranging from those of a niche of sex-positive feminist porn advocates to those of the anti-porn camp of Pamela Paul, Gail Dines, and Shelly Lubben. Perhaps this explains why porn made in the United States by new alternative filmmakers is often characterized by a striking sex-positive pedagogical and political commitment, while cinematically and esthetically it doesn't quite measure up to what we can find in Europe, as we shall see in chapters to follow. While new female porn filmmakers in Europe have the advantage of a more open and relaxed attitude to sexuality and porn than is the case for filmmakers in the United States and Australia, as well as better access to support of the arts, new porn makers in the United States are faced with a cultural context that has a much more conflicted relationship to sex, and little public support for the arts.

Yet, there is still something incredibly cool and promising about what new porn dissenters are making in the United States. Their work often has an edginess and defiance about it that one usually doesn't find in continental sex films, testimony to these American women's bold commitment that gives their porn a unique quality. And of course it is in the United States that you can find the really big porn companies with a lot of money. Some women have teamed up with these for the costs and distribution of their porn, thereby securing their films' higher production value and wider circulation, infiltrating the mainstream market.

The Big Apple: Sexual politics and gender bending porn

The home of Candida Royalle, New York has seen a burgeoning culture of new sex-positive women's voices in the last few years. Candida has taken it upon herself to mentor some of these younger women in the production of feminist sex films. So far she's worked with Jamye Waxman (b. 1974) on *Under the Covers* (2006) and Venus Hottentot, aka Guyanese-American Abiola Abrams (b. 1976), on *AfroDite Superstar* (2007). She is currently in the process of making a second film with Jamye Waxman.

With a Master's in sex education from Widener University, Jamye—the current president of Feminists for Free Expression—shares Candida's sex pedagogical commitment. She is the author of the sex guides *Getting Off: A Woman's Guide to Masturbation* (2007) and *Women Loving Women: Appreciating and Exploring the Beauty of Erotic Female Encounters* (2007), and she has written sex advice columns for among others *Playgirl Magazine*. In 2007, she teamed up with Adam & Eve, Candida's distributor since 1996 and one of a handful of studios that dominate the porn industry in the United States today, for a three-part sex pedagogical video series, *Personal Touch*. One is about using sex toys, another about how to maintain a monogamous relationship without monotony, and the third is about female orgasms. With Adam & Eve's Sensual Couples division she has also produced the educational film *101 Positions for Lovers* (2009).

> *Under the Covers* touches on the wide specter of attitudes to sex in the United States today. We meet a young newlywed couple struggling with shyness when it comes to sex (she in particular), and a female sex therapist who is, on the other hand, quite self-sufficient and pro-active when it comes to pleasuring herself with various sex toys and finding sexual partners online. Interviewed for a television

special about women who are changing the way we think about sex, the therapist explains how she works with her clients, before escorting the reporter to a women-owned sex shop (one of the Babeland shops in New York) where she discusses the benefits of sex toys to women, echoing masturbation educator Betty Dodson.[1] While expressing great interest in the therapist's explanation of various vibrators' functionalities, the journalist is too sheepish to discuss her own favorites ("oh gosh, no, not me; my girlfriends have vibrators, but...").

Refusing the journalist's pleas for an interview, on the other hand, wanting nothing to do with a program that has anything to do with sex, is a certain Monica Young; a spoof on Erica Jong. In her first novel, *Fear of Flying* (1973), Jong coined the "zipless fuck" to describe sex for its own sake, between strangers: "pure" sex free of emotional involvement or commitment.

> The zipless fuck is absolutely pure. It is free of ulterior motives. There is no power game. The man is not "taking" and the woman is not "giving." No one is attempting to cuckold a husband or humiliate a wife. No one is trying to prove anything or get anything out of anyone. The zipless fuck is the purest thing there is.[2]

Resonating at the time with women unhappy with their marriages, many set out to discover free sex for themselves. In recent time, Jong has surprised her followers, however, by stating that "she doubts the pure sexual encounter described in the novel really exists," and arguing that "the best sex, generally, is with somebody where you really have a connection."[3] Now championing the committed marriage, Jong bemoans, however, what she sees as a "cultural trend" saturated by "sterile" sex as women obsess about motherhood and resort to the Internet for "simulated sex without intimacy, without identity and without fear of infection."[4] In *Under the Covers*, we eventually discover that Monica Young in fact has a thing for kink: specifically bondage-play where she is the dominatrix, and group sex. At a sex party in the film's concluding scene, Ms. Young and her husband end up having sex with the reporter; ostensibly there "undercover" for her story.

The film also features a young woman who has pledged her virginity to "Virgins until the Vow." Fanatic about her anti-porn, anti-sex, and anti-masturbation position, she is working undercover for this virginity pledge organization at said sex shop. *Under the Covers* humorously captures how she ultimately succumbs to desire, trying out different sex toys in the backroom after discussing some of the shop's merchandise with the sex therapist. The scene is poignant for there is nothing funny about the movement of virginity pledge programs with their abstinence-until-married trinkets. Pushed for by the same forces that ensured thirty years of federal promotion and funding support for abstinence-only programs, it has fed pubertal hang-ups and warped ideas about sex. After taking office, President Obama has cut most of these funds and introduced new funding initiatives to more effective sex education. It remains to be seen what these positive steps will lead to, however; most schools in the US continue to deprive their students of the benefits of comprehensive human sexuality education.

Though *Under the Covers* is not as successful cinematically as Candida's other films (the acting is a bit stiff, and the lighting and sound quality not as good), it wins in realism, and sex pedagogical and political commitment, addressing both sexual complexes and the cultural hypocrisy in the US towards sex. The film begins with the young couple who've consulted said sex therapist about how to become more comfortable with each other when it comes to sex, especially oral sex. They were both virgins when they married and struggle with insecurities in their sex life; he also worries about the size of his penis. The sex therapist helps him see that the quality of the sex he has with his wife has nothing to do with his penis size, and all about what they do together. She recommends they watch some adult films that also appeal to women and that show loving couples engaging in oral sex since that's a particular issue for them. And she also gives them the assignment to create their own erotic home video to help them become more playful and adventurous with one another. It is this video that they're about to make in the film's opening scene. We see them in their bedroom, alternately through their own video camera that they have set up and through the camera operator's camera. The scenario is realistic: the energy between the two lovers tentative, a bit apprehensive, but also tender and adoring.

AfroDite Superstar is the first in a new line of films from Candida, Femme Chocolat, which promises to deliver films "featuring a more ethnically diverse cast of actors and actresses, directed by women of color." The director in this case is Abiola Abrams, a published writer, television host, and Internet personality. The daughter of highly educated and well-read parents, Abiola grew up in Queens and earned her degrees from reputable writing and arts oriented institutions. She has a Bachelor's from Sarah Lawrence College and a Master's from Vermont College of Fine Arts.

Abiola's feminist art and media outreach focuses especially on empowering women of color. *AfroDite Superstar*—her first porn, or "feminist erotica art film,"[5] as she prefers to call it— reflects Abiola's goal to create a space for women of color to define their sexuality on their own terms and without all the insulting stereotypes that linger around the sexuality of women of color. Abiola directed this film under the pseudonym Venus Hottentot to reclaim the spirit of the real Hottentot Venus: the South African woman Sarah Saartjie Baartman. Born of a Khoisan family in the late eighteen hundreds, Baartman was enslaved by Dutch farmers and exhibited across Europe as an amusement. Her "wild" body—large buttocks and elongated labia typical of some Khoisan women—caused a scandalous sensation among audiences.

With allusions to Spike Lee's *Do the Right Thing* (1989), *AfroDite Superstar* is an intelligent porno-musical that excels cinematically on all levels, delivering strong performances and a terrific soundtrack. The film follows the journey of AfroDite, a young black Beverly Hills woman who wants to become a rap star on her own terms, and is played by Simone Valentino who won a Feminist Porn Award as Best New Star (2007) for this performance. Interspersed throughout the film are compelling home video monologues in which AfroDite finds an outlet for her thoughts and fears, insecurities and longings. Ultimately, her journey brings her to self-acceptance and self-determination, finding it in herself to define who she is rather than allowing others to do it for her.

> *AfroDite Superstar* is particularly successful as afro-empowerment for women, featuring many classic feminist quotes and poetry lines rolling across the screen at opportune moments throughout the film. The musical rap numbers flow naturally within the story, in fact even more so than the sex numbers, which at times feel a bit added-on though well-shot and capturing convincing sexual energy that matches the mood of the scene well. The sex scenes were all co-directed by Candida and reflect her attention to sensuality. The concluding sex scene, which takes place after AfroDite has claimed her identity—deciding to "keep it real," as she puts it in an earlier soliloquy, and be true to herself—is the most powerful, capturing intimacy and chemistry you can feel.

Like Jamye Waxman, Tristan Taormino (b. 1971), founder of Smart Ass Productions (2006), has teamed up with major mainstream porn producers for the production of her films, achieving high production value as a result. First she got Evil Angel onboard for her making of *The Ultimate Guide to Anal Sex for Women I* and *II* (1999, 2001); then Adam & Eve for *House of Ass* (2006). Since 2006, she has collaborated with Vivid Entertainment. First on *Chemistry*: a reality series shot gonzo style, featuring porn stars gathered at a secluded house for a weekend of unscripted sex (4 vols. released to date). Then in 2007 came the first two volumes of Vivid-Ed: Tristan's extensive *Expert Guide* to sex series (15 vols. released to date). And finally, from 2009, *Rough Sex*: a series of episodes that are part documentary and part hardcore erotic vignette, featuring the sexual fantasies of female performers (4 vols. released to date).

Most recently, Tristan made three short instructional porn films (on cunnilingus, fellatio, and the G-spot, all released in

2011) for the sex-positive, progressive, woman-run sex shop Smitten Kitten in Minneapolis. In an educational outreach effort, Smitten Kitten has made these "educational porn" films available for free view online.

Always present in her films, be it by hosting and interviewing or actually demonstrating and performing, Tristan has also acted in feminist porn; specifically in "Not So Tender is the Night" on *Ecstatic Moments* (1999), directed and produced by the Chicago-based feminist academic Marianna Beck and her partner Jack Hafferkamp. With cameo performances by Candida Royalle, Betty Dodson, sexologist Carol Queen and more, Tristan here performs the part of an assured professional woman tackling a sexist, womanizing man head-on. Daring him to take off his clothes on a bare stage in front of all her girlfriends, she teaches him a humbling lesson in sexual etiquette.

For about a decade, Beck and Hafferkamp made a series of Libido Films together that reflect their intellectual and political feminism, confronting double standards and cultural hypocrisy, and a sexual politics that inhibit us sexually. In films like *Ecstatic Moments* (1999), *Urban Friction* (2002), and *Trial Run: Adventures in Romance* (2007) men have to prove that they're not chauvinists, but sensitive and attentive to women's sexual preferences. There's a lot of attention given to clitoral stimulation through cunnilingus and use of sex toys, and the value of role-play is emphasized too. For more than a decade, Beck and Hafferkamp also published the feminist sex positive magazine *Libido: The Journal of Sex and Sensibility*, an intellectual and erotic lifestyle magazine. The couple received significant press in the 1980s when Hafferkamp's tenure track position at the Medill School of Journalism at Northwestern University was terminated because of his work with *Libido*. Beck and Hafferkamp continued to publish the magazine throughout the nineties.[6]

Tristan—who graduated Phi Beta Kappa with a Bachelor's degree in American Studies from Wesleyan University in 1993—

has also obtained solid journalistic experience. She is a former editor of *On Our Backs*, the first women-run magazine to feature lesbian erotica for a lesbian audience in the US; and she served as a syndicated columnist for *The Village Voice* for nearly a decade. Since 1999, she's been writing an advice column for Hustler's *Taboo Magazine*. And she has written several books on sex, and edited numerous erotic anthologies. Her specialty is anal sex. Tristan's first book, *The Ultimate Guide to Anal Sex for Women* (1998) was named Amazon.com's #1 Bestseller in Women's Sex Instruction in 1998. Her first film is based on this book.

Mainstream porn has in recent years degenerated into an excessive focus on extreme anal sex where the goal seems to be to stuff as many penises and fists into the female anus as possible. But sex pedagogical films like Carol Queen's *Bend Over Boyfriend: A Couple's Guide to Male Anal Pleasure* (1998), and Tristan's *Expert Guide to Anal Pleasure for Men* (2009) and her *Expert Guide to Pegging: Strap-on Anal Sex for Couples* (2012) present female-on-male strap-on sex as a sex-positive feminist project where women's active role is advanced and gender differences fade away. Often compared to the female G-spot, the male prostate is surrounded by two bundles of nerves and plays an essential role in ejaculation. Tristan's porn reality series *Chemistry* includes female-on-male strap-on sex among famous porn performers acting in a way you won't see them do in mainstream porn.

Sex workers' rights activist Audacia Ray (b. 1980) confronts the homophobic fear of the male anus head-on in her edgy gender bending porn film *The Bi Apple* (2007). The film follows the young black woman Simone, incidentally the name of this part's performer who also played AfroDite in *AfroDite Superstar*. Simone is a sex researcher (perhaps inspired by Audacia's stint cataloging at the Museum of Sex as a college student) who is on a visit to an apartment called "The Fuckhouse" where open-minded women and men hang out and, well, fuck. With notebook and pen in hand, Simone studies a wide range of different kinds of sex play in the apartment's various rooms.

In one room, Simone meets Tasty Trixie and Tucker Lee (a real life couple who runs the website SpyOnUs.com – "authentic homemade porn"). Trixie and Tucker are sitting cross-legged on the floor meditating; she deeply concentrated, he rather fidgety and impatient. The point, explains Trixie, is to balance the chakras and open the senses to attain even greater sexual pleasure. While Trixie shows a genuine interest in experimenting and expanding their sexual repertoire, Tucker always just wants to be "fucked up the ass." Simone is invited to observe their sex play, which evolves effortlessly the way it does between two lovers intimately familiar with one another.

Trixie and Tucker begin to kiss. Both are in their underwear; he white briefs and T-shirt, dark curls down to his shoulders; she a red chemise with matching lacy panties. She asks him to take it off and finger her. Trixie gets comfortable on her back, lying on a yoga mat with her eyes closed. Tucker lies down next to her, propped up on his elbow, still fingering her and following as the expressions on her face change and the blush on her cheeks gradually darkens. He kisses her nipples. She reaches for a tube of lubrication and applies some herself, before his finger finds its way deep inside her. His cock gets hard; he asks her to feel it. Then she bends over to suck it.

Trixie gets Tucker to turn over onto all four and begins to lick, kiss, and rim his anus, teasing one finger into it; two, three, four. He wants more, turns to look at her; "I think we need that big dildo." She puts on a harness with an erect dark blue dildo and has him lie down on his back; his hips propped up on some pillows, his penis erect on his belly. She penetrates him and pumps him rhythmically this way, before lying down on her back with him on top. He rides the dildo while rocking his hips slightly back and forth, in a way that stimulates her clitoris as well, as she moans contentedly.

Trixi asks Tucker to play with her feet, so he moves down and strokes his penis against her foot; and she asks Simone to hand her a vibrator and a bow shaped kegel dildo. Trixie begins to stimulate her clitoris with the vibrator and the G-spot with the dildo. Tucker continues to tickle her foot with his penis, masturbating until he comes over her breasts, licking off his sperm himself. Then he massages her breasts until she comes with the aids of her vibrator and dildo.

Though Audacia secured Adam & Eve as her film's executive producer and distributor, *The Bi Apple* has a very indie, grassroots feel. Its charm rests in the playful and natural horniness displayed, and the celebration of queer gender bending sexualities; relishing all sorts of sexual appetites, bodies and sex toys. For the film, Audacia won the award for Hottest Bisexual Sex Scene at the Feminist Porn Awards (2007). The film was also nominated for Best Bisexual Release at GayVN Awards, and was screened at Berlin Porn Film Festival (2007) and CineKink NYC (2008).

Art Core: A creative commitment to fluidity, intimacy and sensuality

From German-born UK-based Petra Joy (b. 1964) comes a series of "art-core" films; collections of sensual vignettes characterized by their creative commitment to fluidity and softness even when they feature explicit sex. Candida Royalle recently made available in the US under her Femme Productions label Petra's third film, *Feeling It! Not Faking It...* (2008). As Candida notes, "Joy's work is completely unique and never wavers from her commitment to a feminine vision."[7] Both women were honored as pioneers for their work at the first PorYes! Feminist Porn Film Award Europe in Berlin in 2009.

Petra completed her Master's in Film Studies, Women's Studies, and History at the University of Cologne in 1990. She has a long background as a professional photographer, including doing underwater photography and production of travel and adventure programs for German television. In 1992, she moved to Great Britain because she "wanted to grow creatively and felt [she] could do that better in liberal and experimental England than in conservative Germany," as she put it to me in an email.[8] Indicating her interests in capturing sexy moments on film, she made approximately seventy documentaries for a television show called "Love and Sins" in the following years. And in 2003, she launched Strawberry Seductress; a company catering to women and couples looking for a discreet professional to capture their erotic fantasies in photography, sort of like April in Candida's *My Surrender*, though shooting strictly stills.[9] Then two years later, Petra released her first "art-core" collection. Three have followed. *Feeling It!* is the third installment.

Petra was originally opposed to porn making, however. She recounts when the anti-porn movement kicked off in the 80s. At the time a film student, she wanted to make up her own mind. So she rented several porn films to analyze their content:

All of the films I saw were misogynist and violent (with words or actions) towards women. The films left me with a bad taste. I was angry to see women being humiliated and hurt (one film featured the ripping of a woman's nipple with barb wire) and decided I was against this kind of porn. At the time it was important for me to say "No" and draw a boundary.

But with time I began to wonder: Why should we leave the production of erotic and pornographic images solely in male hands? Why should women not create and enjoy films that express their sexual desires and inspire and arouse them? This limits us and excludes us from expressing our fantasies on film and exploring our sexuality. I now enjoy saying "Yes." I create alternatives porn films that focus on what women want.[10]

As a whole, Petra's films reflect her artistic vision. Explains Petra:

The focus of my erotic films is female pleasure. ... I feel the need to create an alternative to the flood of images that reduce women to their genitals.

I believe in a return to sensuality and portray a sex play that is enriched by intimacy, creativity and humour. I love to show women being caressed and receiving oral sex as we do not see enough of this. ...

I also like to show men as objects of female sexual desires as there is a lack of male pin-up culture that is aimed at women rather than gay men in our culture. I choose to embrace taboo subjects such as male bisexuality and the prostate as an erogenous zone for (heterosexual) men.

I call my films art-core, rather than hard-core. Even though I do feature erections, penetration and show "real sex," I do not feel I have much in common with 90% of films in the genre of hard-core porn. I am an artist and enjoy making sensuality the subject of my visual experimental art.[11]

About an hour long, *Feeling It!* contains eight unrelated vignettes, all without dialog, and instead accompanied by sensuous and sexy rhythms.

The collection begins with a series of close-ups of lips and skin that are painted by brush strokes, creating sensual contrasts before and as they are touched, licked, and kissed; many by explicit invitation. "Lick me!" say the words painted on a woman's torso with an arrow pointing down towards her pussy. On a man's abdomen, the sign "use me" is painted with an arrow pointing down towards his penis.

Next is a vignette featuring a woman dressed in white old-fashioned underwear standing on a balcony with her back facing us, gazing at the blue sky, puffy white clouds and seagulls flying. An "angel" — a man in white thong and white feather wings — comes down to her, leans up close to her from behind, caresses her hair, her back; kisses her. On her back are faint lines drawing the contours of wings as if she once had wings there too. The crack on her thin white knickers reveals her anus; he fondles it. They embrace and then he licks her pussy. And again. In the end, he penetrates her from behind before lifting his arms up in the air to fly away. She gazes up after him.

The next vignette features three women: two dressed in sailor boy costumes and smoking cigars, the third in a cabaret outfit with high heels and long red gloves. She is handcuffed and pleasured in multiple ways by the two sailor boy-girls. The picture remains soft with warm red walls and dark purple satin sheets. The two sailor girls, each equipped with a black dildo as it turns out, at one point begin to kiss. And then all their tongues and limbs and lips are eventually intertwined as their circle of pleasuring moves between them.

A man hot in the sun from mowing strips down to his underwear in this vignette while still mowing the lawn and before hosing himself down and then masturbating, lounging in the sun. Sexy close-ups capture the muscles of his arm flexing, his lips moving as he speaks on his cell phone, his hand stroking his cock, faster; the head of his cock shining as he comes; he licks his lips.

My favorite vignette follows, featuring the mutual exploration of the bodies of a white woman and a black man. He begins by stroking her with a feather; then she begins to stroke and discover him. She tickles him with her pearls and lace lingerie; drips massage oil over him, then lies down on top of him.

The sexual energy moving, the music shifts to a rhythmic trance pop club music as the tension mounts and she begins to photograph him lying naked on his back in bed. Then he, helped by her, stimulates her with a slick silvery dildo while caressing her breasts, pinching her nipples. He licks her, she him. She takes his cock in her hands and massages it as he continues to lick her pussy. And penetrates her with the silvery dildo as both face the camera, capturing the pleasure in her face. Then in one of the most sexiest scenes ever introducing a condom, she wraps one over his cock, helping with her mouth. Sucks him. Then rides him. He rides her, comes — then she while helping with her hand.

The next scene features a woman dressed in a tight black dress and high heels, sitting in a red leather chair by the fireplace of a mansion's library. Next to her is a side table with a glass of white wine and a lowball with some ice cubes. She sips her wine, leafing through the pages of an old leather-bound book, its pages yellowing, featuring kinky illustrations. Then she lifts up the receiver of a phone, dials a number, and utters a formal "come over and serve me." Repeats it. A man arrives. Wearing black chaps that that reveal his buttocks and crotch, he is otherwise naked. He bends down and kisses her feet, exposing his buttocks. She takes an ice cube from her lowball, strokes it down his naked back, tickling his butt with it while he's leaning over her legs, still kissing her feet. Then she teases it up along her own legs; and he follows it with his licks. The two kiss.

The rhythm shifts to a faster darker beat; he licks her pussy. She lays him down over her lap and lightly spanks his bum and licks his buttocks before ever so gently teasing a finger into his anus. She penetrates him with her fingers while he himself strokes his cock; she then penetrates him with a black butt plug while she also strokes his cock. Eventually he penetrates her while she helps with her fingers. They finish with him penetrating her from behind as she rocks her hips before they linger in embrace, kissing as the picture fades out.

The following vignette is filmed in black and white: a woman in a garden is lounging in a wicker chair, reading while holding a parasol shading the sun. At one point, she sets the parasol aside and begins to touch herself. A woman wearing only delicate underwear approaches from behind, puts her hands over the woman's eyes; kisses her. A mutual exchange of naked pleasuring follows. The entire vignette is filled with a series of floating intimate shots from alluring camera angles, and the pictures bleed in and out of one another, filtered by the patterns of the parasol and the shadows and shapes in the garden.

The final scene features a group of girlfriends in party mood at a select lounge. They order champagne and are so served by a man, naked except for a black apron. They slap his bum teasingly and toast with champagne, giving and sharing kisses. Bent over, another man's naked back serves as a tray for the sushi the women are served next. They feed each other while stroking the man's buttocks with their chopsticks and fingers. The women ring the bell again; a silver plate of oysters arrives. They toast with the oysters. Strawberries shimmering with glossy glitter follow. Hungry for more, their teasing play with the server's body becomes more charged as they savor and explore his naked body, lifting the apron aside. Then a black man dressed in tuxedo pops out of a big gift box and an erotic orgy between the women and the servers ensue to the heat of a jazzy beat.

Included as an extra is the porn parody "Girls & Vegetables;" a spoof on mainstream hard core that highlights how different Petra's art core is from it, in this case as it pertains to the featuring of girl-girl sex.

Concluding the collection's credits is a quotation from Wolfgang Amadeus Mozart: "I pay no attention whatever to anybody's praise or blame. I simply follow my own feelings."

And indeed: powerful behind-the-scenes documentaries included on Petra's DVDs demonstrate Petra's very compelling intentions and creativity while working with fairly limited resources. How much she herself actually moves with her camera around the actors as she films them to achieve the flow she seeks; how she plays with canvases, curtains, parasols, and more to create soft and artistic filters; how she comes up with creative ideas for more arty shots; how she shoots in very simple settings that she then adds more onto in post-production. On the documentaries, we also get to see how everyone from the staff and even cast pitches in to help with everything from make-up to props, sets, and lighting. A democratic project indeed, as Petra herself underscores.

On that note, Petra also deserves recognition for her outreaching efforts inspiring other women to get involved behind the camera with their new visions. As Petra points out:

> It is important that more and more of us get behind the camera to make our visions of sexuality seen and heard. ... Only 6% of Hollywood directors are female. This percentage is even smaller when it comes to the porn industry. What this means is that most films show us life from a male perspective. I would like to adjust the balance, and I want to empower women to show us what is erotic to them.[12]

With that in mind, Petra created the Petra Joy Awards, to "encourage newcomers and look into the future so that the genre will continue to thrive."[13] She invited women around the world to submit their work featuring what is erotic to them and assembled a jury of qualified women to judge the short films. The results were announced at the first Petra Joy Awards, which were held in conjunction with Berlin Porn Film Festival in 2009. The winner, Louise Lush's *That's What I Like* (2009), and the follow-up films were then included on Petra's *Her Porn* Volume II (2010). Sponsored by Pjur, a manufacturer of health and body care products, the winners also received prize money. Volume I of *Her Porn* (2009) is a compilation of short films and clips from porn made by women over the last decade. A third compilation was released in 2011.

* * *

Feeling It! was originally conceived as *More Female Fantasies*: a follow-up to Petra's second release *Female Fantasies*, which premiered at the first Berlin Porn Film Festival in 2006 and for which Petra won the award for Most Erotic Film at Barcelona International Erotic Film Festival (2007). Like its sequel, it is approximately an hour long and contains a series of unrelated short erotic vignettes. The vignettes integrate arty shots of food play, esthetic sex toys, lush feather displays, eroticized acrobatic underwater swimming, shades of deep scarlet, burlesque silhouettes and more art-core effects while portraying the erotic fantasies that were sent to Petra by her female photography clients and friends. (The scenarios in *Feeling It!* are also based on erotic fantasies that women shared with Petra.)

With a focus on women being pleasured, the collection also includes an extremely sexy vignette shot in black-and-white featuring a man masturbating in the shower. Esthetic close-ups of skin, curves, a finger tickling his nipple as the man gently strokes his cock charge this scene. This collection also includes a vignette that is intriguing for how it explores male bisexuality within a heterosexual context; this vignette was awarded Best Bi Scene at the Feminist Porn Award (2008). And whereas a woman is shown being pleasured while blindfolded, one vignette also features a man blindfolded and pleasured by his female partner.

The half-hour long *Sexual Sushi* (2004), Petra's first film, is also flavored by her art-core sensuous style of esthetics and a penchant for soft red lighting, but in contrast to the other collections, this one follows one couple in three different erotic scenarios, including one in which she is blindfolded while stimulated and served, another featuring their tongue-in-cheek erotic role-play, and finally a romantic bath the lovers share. A fourth segment portrays her girl-sex fantasy. The short films are bookended by an extravaganza of colored lights and silhouettes of couples kissing, licking and touching each other, sensually rocking bodies, a woman moving glowing red and green lights over her body, naked fire twirlers spinning brazing flames over exposed flesh.

Petra departs from the vignette format in her latest installment, the 75-minute long film *The Female Voyeur* (2011), which is devoted to women who like to gaze at men and call the shots. In particular, the film illustrates some key tenets of Petra's creative vision, including the featuring of men as the objects of female sexual desire, male bisexuality, and men devoted to sexually pleasing women. The first episode features a female photographer taking pictures of and seducing two male models before they all have sex through a series of positions against a red backdrop. The second episode is more playfully shot as a talent show with three men taking turns performing in front of an all-female jury whom they take turn pleasuring. The final episode is staged as a Roman orgy accompanied by a Middle Eastern inspired soundtrack. By far the longest episode, it is nevertheless the one that most resembles Petra's previous art-core work with flowing camera movements and creative shots through curtains and bedrails, the images softly dissolving in and out of one another. Framing a large bed covered by red sheets and the naked bodies of a group of women and men, the episode dwells on the enmeshment of flesh and limbs where it becomes unclear who's being pleasured by whom; where the message instead conveyed is that at least in this case, it doesn't matter who pleasures whom. The first part of this episode focuses entirely on the lovers' sensual massage and pleasuring of one woman. *The Female Voyeur* won Steamiest Straight Movie at the Feminist Porn Awards (2012).

Vanilla Sex: Objecting to double standards

Louise Lush who won first prize at the first Petra Joy Awards, is better known as the feminist sex and porn-for-women blogger Ms. Naughty, who is also the Webmistress behind the largest domain network of porn aimed at women. Ms. Naughty (b. 1973) who lives and works out of a small town in Australia, is a former librarian and freelance journalist. Her work stands out for the consistent quality of her writing and the informed sex-positive feminist commitment she displays in both her texts and films, despite, or perhaps further provoked by, Australia's strict regulation of porn under which she's working. Not only is it illegal to maintain porn sites on Australian servers (Ms. Naughty uses American servers); the production of porn film is either illegal or strictly regulated, depending on the state; and it is illegal to sell or rent out "objectionable" films, though it is legal to buy or own them.[14] For these reasons, Ms. Naughty has considered moving to Europe or the United States with her husband. It is also why I am not providing her real name. At the time of writing, the Australian government is reviewing its censorship regime, admitting that it no longer functions in a meaningful way.

In 1999, while working on an article about online porn for women, Ms. Naughty found such sites to be practically non-existent. For the article she had contacted the woman who ran Purve.com ("gurls purve too")—the first women's porn site, launched only the year before—and was later convinced by her to get into the business. In 2000, Ms. Naughty launched her sex column Grandma Scrotum's Sex Tips; her Ms. Naughty blog covering news about sex, censorship, erotica, and porn has been active since 2004; and by 2006 she owned 120 domains, including her pay-to-subscribe ezine For the Girls that features articles, reviews, erotic stories, pictures, and videos. Ms. Naughty also runs several websites where she sells selected porn films for a female audience, and in 2008 she established Indigo Lush Media and began making porn under the name Louise Lush.

Ms. Naughty makes it clear on her sites that her content is directed to a mainstream heterosexual female audience. As she explains to me in an email:

When I first started out, the customer I had in mind was "hetero women." Over the years I've discovered that Ms.

Hetero Woman does not necessarily exist. I'm aware that most of my sites cater to Ms. Hetero Suburban White Woman with Fairly Vanilla Tastes. That's who I am, so I know my market.[15]

This is also the case for the porn she makes, as she explains on her Indigo Lush website:

While Indigo Lush is accepting of all forms of sexuality including queer identities and kink, we're also very keen on presenting "vanilla" eroticism without all the usual porn clichés. This is because this idea of sex is still rarely explored by filmmakers — even among the new wave of "indie" porn producers. Vanilla is often dismissed as too boring or mainstream to explore and yet it's the way the majority of people make love. We want to create films where "ordinary" sex is honored as the sensual, intimate and powerful thing we all know it to be.[16]

Objecting to sexual double standards, Ms. Naughty is committed to encouraging women to take charge of their sexuality and be active about communicating their sexual preferences. In her first film, the ten-minute short *That's What I Like* (2009), she implicitly instructs women on how to do so. The film crosscuts between an interview with the female porn performer Mia about her sexual preferences and a scene featuring Mia having her choice of sex, with the action matching her descriptions. In an expanded version, Mia's sexual partner Andy is also interviewed about his sexual preferences.

In line with Indigo Lush's vanilla focus, Mia expresses fairly traditional preferences: such as missionary position ("because then I don't need to do anything," she grins) though she also likes variation. She likes to begin with kissing, especially along the neck, and a little massage. She likes to use sex toys, both alone and with a partner, to be on top, and to finish in "doggy" because then she can more easily help stimulate her clitoris with her own fingers. But she actually prefers to come when someone is giving her oral sex, because that feels more intense to her. — Ms. Naughty often returns in her writing to how fed up she is with all the focus on blowjobs in mainstream porn and popular media, demanding attention to the fact that women too enjoy receiving oral sex.

Mia and Andy, who know each other from previous jobs, have a good connection and chemistry. He smiles warmly to her when giving her oral sex, and when in turn she is giving him oral sex. The camera zooms in on her hand reaching for his as he licks her, then she pulls him up to where they kiss and embrace. The film does not include a money shot to "prove" his climax; only from their facial expressions, sighs, and moans do we get that they come; he in the doggy style that she likes, she while receiving oral sex afterwards.

True to Mia's expressed preferences, we see her mostly lying on her back; her long brown hair spread out on the pillow as his blond ruffled hair gets moist by his temples, his face flushed. But Mia does go down on Andy and rides him too. The sexiest scene is when Andy uses a vibrator to stimulate Mia: the close-ups of him applying lubrication on her pussy; caressing and tickling her open labia; then fingering her, before stimulating and penetrating her with the vibrator. The expanded version shows that it is in fact Mia who pulls out the vibrator, asking Andy to use it on her; explicitly expressing her sexual preference to him.

That's What I Like is a small budget production made with attention to stylistic details. The interview features Mia sitting on a red leather couch, red-pink walls around her, sunshine beaming in through a window in the background. The sex is shot in a blue-lit room, black walls, sheets, and floor, some violet shawls draped over the head- and footboards. There is no added soundtrack, except for at the end when a romantic guitar melody enters the picture of the two cuddling in bed while the credits scroll over the screen. Other than that, we only hear their panting, kissing, licking, sighing and slight moaning, eventually also the bed squeaking, and some traffic outside.

For *That's What I Like* Ms. Naughty (as Louise Lush) won first prize at the women oriented Petra Joy Awards in 2009 (presented in conjunction with Berlin Porn Film Festival) for its focus on female pleasure. Louise also released a three-minute long promotional film for her ezine in 2009, *Paddling the Pink Canoe*, a humorous catalogue of the numerous euphemisms for female masturbation. For as she states on her website, women's masturbation is still a very taboo topic. By talking about it, we bring it out of the closet.

In 2011, Louise completed the three-minute short film *Fucking Is The Only Prayer* (2011), a sensual look at the spiritual side of sex, featuring an actual married couple with no former experience in porn. The film uses close-up images of sex combined with religious music to invoke a spiritual atmosphere devoted to the idea that the body is our temple. It screened at CineKink NYC (2011) and was nominated for a Feminist Porn Award (2011).

Louise's short film *The Thought Of Her* also premiered in 2011, in this case at Berlin Porn Film Festival. Featuring a man masturbating as we follow his internal monologue—the thought of her—the film strives to capture some of the mental processes involved in self-pleasure. Similar in style to *Fucking Is The Only Prayer*, the film uses an effective cross lighting with a black background, and lingers on powerfully meaningful close-ups: his eyes closing, his tongue licking his lips, his toes curling inwards, his upper arm pulsing, his fingers clenching, his forehead contracting.

I.M. In Love is Louise's latest short film. A playful look at instant messaging and cybersex within the context of a relationship, it premiered at CineKink NYC (2012). Louise also completed her first long length film in 2012. Titled *The Thought Of Her* like the original short film, it features four male masturbation scenes as well as interviews with the men. Currently, Louise is developing an erotic feature film titled *The Garden*, which promises to have a psychological vibe as it explores a collection of real women's fantasies that range in content from the romantic to the taboo breaking, all depicted in vignettes within an overarching storyline.

Chapter 5

Modern Music Video Porn: A Fresh Artistic Edge

In the early eighties, while MTV was still a fresh concept, Candida Royalle introduced the "erotic rock video."[1] Today, the erotic rock video format is revitalized and modernized by a new generation of women with a fresh perspective and a new artistic edge. They are situated in Europe where they benefit from a greater openness to sex and progressive porn, as well as more support for the arts. With backgrounds ranging from fashion and design to photography and media art, they collaborate with upscale design companies and see their work featured at reputable film festivals and even prestigious art institutes.

Lust Films: MTV porn for modern urbanites

Swedish-born Erika Lust (b. 1977) who lives and works in Barcelona, Spain is at the forefront of this modern movement of arty progressive porn. Her focus is on realistic scenarios presented in short films of high quality, shot in the style of music videos with hip editing and catchy soundtracks. As she herself puts it, her porn speaks to a generation that grew up with MTV and shows like *Sex and the City*.

Erika, who has a Bachelor's in political science from Lund University where she also studied feminist theory, describes as follows how she got into this business:

> It was anything but love at first sight. Obviously, there was something about the images that turned me on, but there were also a lot of things that bothered me.
>
> I couldn't see myself in those films—not my lifestyle or my values, and not my sexuality. ... But even though I didn't like

what I was seeing, something inside me was pushing me to look deeper. ... I understood that a different kind of porn was possible, and that women had a great deal to contribute to a genre that had always been the exclusive province of men.[2]

Eventually, in 2004, Erika made her first explicit short film: the twenty-minute long *The Good Girl*. Breaking with formulaic mass-produced mainstream porn, she was, however, unable to find anyone to distribute it for her. Finally, in the spring of 2006, she launched a blog and made her film available as a free download there under a Creative Commons license. In her blog, she posted about how hopeless porno moguls can be to work with (Erika had insider experience from her freelance work as technical assistant and location manager for various companies, including the huge porn company Private), and how difficult it is to penetrate the market when you produce something that truly differs from what they make. She wrote about the predictable nature of porn made by men, and the need for a new kind of porn for women. Finally, she sent out an announcement for her work over email. I received it via the owner of a woman-run sex shop called Lust in Copenhagen with whom I had recently been in touch about the selection of films sold in her store.

Firstly, Erika shows definite skills in film techniques. She has a good eye for picture composition and editing, with a style and rhythm that can appeal to modern urban people today. I immediately connected with her work, not only because I could identify with the main character in *The Good Girl*, but also because I was grabbed by Erika's use of music and the cinematic quality.

In *The Good Girl* we get to know a young woman, Alexandra who, despite a rich erotic fantasy life (of which the audience gets a few comical glimpses), struggles to give in to her sexual fantasies. Her friend Julie, on the other hand, seems to have no problems in that department at all. Alexandra's frustration and exasperation over her friend's lack of understanding is captured with a good dose of humor and self-irony.

The film begins with a phone conversation between the two friends. In the background we hear a lively upbeat music; there's a happy hour feel over the scene. Julie is in the midst of a hectic work environment. Her office flooded by the afternoon sunlight, she is busy calling out last minute instructions. Alexandra, on the other hand, has just gotten home to the peace and quiet of her studio apartment, warmed by the color of the red brick walls. She kicks off her shoes onto the hard wooden floor and pours herself a glass of red wine. In the meantime, Julie's going on and on about her newest sexual adventure with her yoga instructor. Alexandra asks if it wasn't a tai chi teacher Julie was seeing, but apparently that was so last week. Julie continues with a detailed description of the sex they had—of which we get a few telling quick shots—while Alexandra looks into the camera with a "see what I mean?" look. She tells us how she wishes she too could be "more daring" and do "something not expected of a good girl like me." How she sometimes fantasizes about her massage therapist going all the way down on her, or making a pass on the construction worker. Or doing what they always do in porn, like when the pizza guy comes to deliver the pizza and the girl drops the towel because of course she just had a shower. But, she sighs; in real life pizza guys are not exactly gorgeous handsome models. Before hanging up, Alexandra tells Julie she's tired, she needs a shower, wants to order pizza and just relax at home for the night.

The Good Girl is about how Alexandra overcomes her hang-ups so she can enjoy—on her own terms—her body and sexuality, with, ironically, a pizza deliverer. When he arrives in the next scene, he is for once incredibly handsome! And of course, she has just had a shower and is wearing only a towel wrapped around her body. After some awkward fumbling around to find money to pay for the pizza, and he's safely out of sight, she sinks down on the floor against the shut door, frustrated with herself. But then the doorbell rings again. She resolutely opens the door, looks intently into his eyes, and then she throws her arms around his neck and hugs him. "Eh, I forgot my helmet," he stutters in response. It's comical, embarrassing, and heartbreaking all at the same time, but it has to be now or never; she lets the towel fall, peeking up at him. And in an instantaneous connection, he *sees* her.

And here enters the film's musical soundtrack, first light tender keystrokes on the piano that suggest where things might go. Eventually the music picks up into a lively pop melody, escalating in synch with their sex as the passion between them soars. And of course the two are beautiful to look at. He dark, almost Italian-like, but in a charming, unthreatening, and kind sort of way; she sweet in a natural manner, with long soft blond hair and smooth skin over her supple body. The rhythm in the editing and music works all throughout, and you can feel it in your body. We follow and feel with Alexandra from the first fumbling and uncertain touches, to the burning fever that takes over the brain when reason must let go. She does let go, receiving and giving; their sex a passionate life-affirming dance that lifts her up and carries her away. "Fire! ... I feel fire!" exclaims the vocalist as she rises up, full of desire, into a tense arching bow of pleasure. The film reaches its climax as she comes, and then everything settles down before she tells him with a mischievous smile, "I want you to come in my face like in porn movies!" And when he does, it only looks creamy and delicate.

In the final moments of the film the two introduce themselves to each other before sharing the cold pizza, talking and laughing. He writes his number on the empty pizza box before kissing her goodbye; an invitation to a continuation. So it's not necessarily a one-nighter, but even if it is, they've had a connection, they've seen one another, given to each other; it's meant something to them. Dropping that towel changed my life, reflects Alexandra in voiceover; "somehow that moment was my liberation ... of not always doing what's expected of a 'good girl' like me," she concludes as the picture fades out.

At the time Erika posted *The Good Girl* online, I was on sabbatical in Norway researching feminist pornography. I immediately sent a link for the video to the leading sex-positive retailer there (Cupido), which soon became Erika's first vendor. Not long after, the free download option went away. By then it had been downloaded two million times.

That summer Erika attended the "Good Porn" event I organized in Oslo with Cupido. Over good dinners and wine, and while touring the city in the bright summer light, we shared our feminist dreams and aspirations, and our own personal stories. Bombarded from a young age by a popular media that told us our bodies weren't measuring up, we had also both experienced the discomfort that lingers around sex — even in so-called sexually liberated and gender equal Scandinavia. We discussed the politics of sex in our culture, and the conflicting young feminisms of raunch critic Ariel Levy and the porn screening sex parties of CAKE (a euphemism for women's genitalia), which were both in the air at the time. While Levy was criticizing porn for its plastic and "fixed" depiction of sex, the founders of the CAKE movement, Melinda Gallagher and Emily Scarlet Kramer, argued that there simply hasn't been produced enough porn "tailored to the female eye."[3]

Eventually Erika terminated her first blog and developed a professional website for her film company Lust Films & Publications of Barcelona, which she runs with her Spanish partner Pablo Dobner. Together the two have since produced *Five Hot Stories for Her* (2007), *Barcelona Sex Project* (2008), *Life, Love, Lust* (2010), and *Cabaret Desire* (2011). The two have also become the parents of two daughters. On her new blog, Erika continues to post about the politics of sex and porn from a feminist perspective, and now also that of a mom, addressing issues of pertinent interest to women who care about ending the perpetu-ation of gender stereotypes and sexual discrimination fed by popular culture, pornified media, and mainstream porn. Posting on the new Twilight Saga movie *Breaking Dawn*, for instance, a film based on the best-selling book by the same name—which *The Independent* criticized as "shockingly, tackily, sick-makingly sexist" with a main female character that "lives to serve men and suffer"[4]—Erika writes in her blog:

It's all that I fight against. It goes **against every feminist principle**. I will keep doing what I do so that there aren't any more appalling movies like this one when my daughters grow up, because I certainly don't want them to grow up with the idea that their goal in life is to find a guy at 17, get married to then have sex and then immediately get pregnant. It's so sad to need to remind people that a woman can be someone without a man! **This gender stereotyping is seriously what's wrong in our society** and having to suffer this kind of old-minded product **makes me want to make as much feminist porn as I can!**[5]

To the London-based magazine *Filament: "For Women Who Like Hot Men and Intelligent Thought,"* Erika recently summarized her view on porn as follows:

I see porn as a tool for excitement, education and pleasure. It's not only an entertainment product, but also a powerful way to influence future generations' vision of human sexuality. That's why I think women have to take part in the political discourse of porn: if we don't participate, porn will not be an expression of human sexuality, but an expression of male sexuality.[6]

Five Hot Stories for Her, which includes "The Good Girl," is, as the title implies, a collection of five short porn films aimed at a female audience, expressing the sexuality of modern women and men. In addition to "The Good Girl," we get to see how the dark beautiful tattooed and long-haired Nadia, who works in a sex toy shop, fascinates various women, lesbian as well as hetero ("Something about Nadia"); how the hip young wife Sonja catches her professional soccer player husband Carlos having sex in their bed with another woman, and gets even by having sex with two of her husband's teammates, recording it on video and uploading it to the Internet ("Jodetecarlos.com"); how a married couple with children maintains the spark in their relationship by having a weekly BDSM-date in another apartment, while a babysitter watches the kids at their home ("Married with children"); and, instead of the typical girl-sex episode in mainstream porn, Erika concludes this collection with a break-up sex scene between two men in the stylish apartment they've shared until now, shot in artistic black-and-white ("Breakup sex").

All the short films are characterized by Erika's meticulous filmic techniques. The photography is professional and slick with an attention-grabbing use of angles; the editing energetic, even electrifying, creating a sexy teasing rhythm, which the hip music further underscores. Erika tantalizes the viewer with images floating by: short glimpses of skin, form, pussy, nipple. Without lingering on the explicit, the focus of each shot is on the esthetics. It is modern with women and men in an urban setting: Barcelona with its well-known Gaudi architecture, plazas and avenues, shopping streets, café corners, ultramodern apartments, the long beach. Originally shot in Spanish—except for "The Good Girl" where the actors speak English with a charming accent—the dubbing on the English version gives the short films a bit of a corny feel at times. Still, for *Five Hot Stories for Her*, Erika won the awards for Best Manuscript at Barcelona International Erotic Film Festival 2007, *The Good Girl* won a prize for Best Short Film at this festival in 2005, Best Film of the Year at the Feminist Porn Awards (2008), and Honorable Best Mention at CineKink NYC (2008).

Since releasing *Five Hot Stories for Her*, Erika has fine-tuned her erotic filmmaking skills. With *Life, Love, Lust*, a collection of three short films capturing captivating scenarios between attractive characters, Erika delivers polished quality with high production value. The rhythm captures and matches the story well, while photography and editing are stylistically striking and seamless at the same time. None of the films are dubbed. What we hear of dialog in the background (in Spanish) adds depth to the picture, but is not essential to understanding the story.

The first film ("Life") captures the workday of a waitress and her boyfriend, a chef at the same restaurant, through quick crosscuts. The two close up the restaurant at the end of the shift, and sit down for a drink in the bar to celebrate his birthday before having sex there too. Then they have cake and she gives him a gift: a telling pregnancy test. Whereas "Life" has a warm sexy stylish feel to it, "Love" is filled with both the nostalgia of falling in love and the melancholy of a broken heart, as it portrays in dreamy shots the affair between a married business-woman and a sensitive guitar-playing younger man. And in "Lust" we follow the torn journey of a seeking but hesitant dark young woman who in the end seeks out a shorthaired tattooed masseuse for tantric massage and release.

Life, Love, Lust also comes with the erotic film noir vignette "Handcuffs" where a woman in an art deco nightclub observes another woman in handcuffs serving her male partner. The vignette is written and directed by Erika with photography by Gustavo Lópes Mañas. It premiered at the Erotic Night at the short film festival Circuito Off in Venice (2009), later winning Best Experimental Short Film at CineKink NYC (2010), and Sexiest Short Film of the Year (2010) at the Feminist Porn Awards. The playful short film "Love Me Like You Hate Me" about domination and submission between two English-speaking ladies also comes as an extra. For Life, Love, Lust, Erika won the award for Movie of the Year at the Feminist Porn Awards (2011).

Barcelona Sex Project is different from Erika's other work in both content and style. Shot as a documentary featuring three women and three men, we first get a sense of their everyday lives and likes through one-on-one interviews, before we see them masturbate individually for the camera. Both the interviews and the masturbation scenes are shot in a more subdued style than Erika's short films, further emphasized by the white backdrop and minimalist furniture used for this documentary.

As an example of the rising respect and cultural mainstreaming of artistic and feminist sex films, Erika—together with five other directors—was in 2010 invited by the innovate production house boolab to shoot a short film using the ultra-hip international shoe company Camper's boutique hotel in Barcelona, Casa Camper, as its setting. In February of 2011, the *Hotel Casa Camper* movie premiered for free view online: hotel-casacamper.tv. Erika's "Room 33" is the third of six shorts and reprises the roles of the couple from "Handcuffs" as they check into a hotel charged with erotic atmosphere, which is tantalizingly captured in quick spinning flashbacks to their previous erotic stays at the same hotel. The film received an Honorable Best Mention at CineKink NYC (2011).

Both "Handcuffs" and "Room 33" are included on Erika's latest film, *Cabaret Desire*. More mature and unhurried in its feel, Erika here adds a new touch to her modern and urban *Sex and the City* styled porn. Inspired by an actual New York Poetry Brothel and its Barcelona sister branch, both founded by poets fresh out of university and desiring a more intimate, creative outlet for their work,[7] the film elicits the lush burlesque feel of *fin-de-siècle* Europe with its bohemian free-love poets and artists. Inviting the viewer in the opening scene into a vintage nightclub packed with atmosphere—the music tense and vibrating with energy as a man in leotard spins around a pole—we are promised an evening full of passion, dance, music, and erotic readings from poets who will seduce and delight with tales of intimate erotica, evocative imageries and much more.

Narrated by actual poetry "whores" who are skilled at reciting their work on an intimate one-on-one basis to their "clients," the film includes four stories. Each of them begins in the "brothel"—a lavish dimly lit nightclub where the poet retreats to a quiet corner for his or her reading— before sexy and seductive illustrations of the poet's story fill the screen.

With each short story, Erika delivers more of her modern and urban slickly styled porn with characters that are all very attractive, donning sexy taboos and their own individualized styles. None of them abide by the porny ideals of commercial media and nothing of what we see them do has the look or feel of mainstream porn. Barcelona's urban architecture with its chic bars and cafés is well incorporated.

In terms of content, the film makes a point of featuring strong women who refuse to fit labels or abide by conventions, be it the short-haired lushly bodied woman who, tired of having to define herself, simultaneously pursues an affair both with a woman and also with a man, and without telling either, or a poet's mother, radical in her time for her pursuit of counter culture as a painter and an art historian, and also as a single mother.

The third story features a modern young woman surrounded by good friends. In the opening scene, she reflects on how different her life has turned out from how she pictured it as a young girl when she thought she'd grow up to embrace a life with "a fulfilling career, a handsome and adoring husband, two kids and a dog." But how our "white picket fantasies" change as we transform and become who we are. Instead of marrying, she's pursued a life of freedom, sexually too.

The final story follows a woman on her way to a date with a handsome and divorced dark-haired man who is also a dad; we see him biking through the streets with a child seat on his bike. Featuring more of Barcelona's city landscape, the film charmingly captures the insecurities of both the woman and the man before "a first date."

Also included as a bonus material on *Cabaret Desire* is a documentary on the poetry brothels. Featuring interviews with some of the poetry "whores," we learn more about the way they work and why: how they embrace reading their work on a one-on-one basis as it allows them not only the opportunity to convey the attitude and voice intended to their audiences, but also a unique intimate interaction with them.

Cabaret Desire had its US premiere as the official opening film of CineKink NYC (2012) where it tied for the Audience Choice Award for Best Narrative Feature. It won Movie of the Year at the Feminist Porn Awards (2012).

Erika has also written several books, including *Good Porn: A Woman's Guide* (2010), an introductory user guide to porn that features a smorgasbord of Erika's recommended films, and *The Erotic Bible to Europe: From Kinky to Chic* (2010), a travel guide to erotic destinations in Europe. She co-authored *Love Me Like You Hate Me: Lessons in Pleasure and Pain* (2010), a sex guide to fetish play and BDSM, with Venus O'Hare who also performs in the film by the same name.[8]

I make porn and I love it: Music video art from La Fille d'O

Murielle Scherre (b. 1977) is the woman behind the ultra hip Belgium-based lingerie company La Fille d'O. Founded in 2003, its circle of customers has grown to include numerous famous music artists from across the world, including Lady Gaga, Robyn, Roísín Murphy, Juliette Lewis, and M.I.A. In her manifesto for La Fille d'O (which she spells out as "libertine, animal, footloose, indulgent, legendary, long-term, electric, determined, and oddly overwhelming"), Murielle fleshes out the ethics and aspirations of her company, which she sums up as "a daily revolution from the underbelly of fashion."[9] With collections that now also include shoes, jewelry, and more, in addition to Murielle's vintage inspired, upscale lingerie, La Fille d'O has in fact come to represent a lifestyle concept. Online, La Fille d'O features Murielle's sexy, untouched up photo, video, and poetry art; in part modeling merchandise, in part an extension of her re-visioned porn. The author of two sexual memoirs, Murielle also models her own work.

Murielle's first porn film, *J'fais du porno et j'aime ça* (I make porn and I love it), was originally distributed as a supplement to the 2009 August issue of the popular Belgian lifestyle magazine *Goedele*. The film is now available from La Fille d'O, but its original release is interesting as yet another example of the growing cultural acceptance and appreciation of artistic progressive sex films. The magazine's founder, Goedele Liekens (b. 1963), has in fact done much to bring attention to women's re-visioned porn beyond distributing Murielle's film. A former Miss Belgium (1986), Goedele is a high-profiled media person, known for her outspoken opinions, including on sex and porn.

"Why make porn these days, you wonder?" asks Murielle, before answering as follows in the manifesto for her porn spelled out on the inside of her DVD's cover:

I hold nothing against porn itself. What does make my skin creep is the total lack of the pure basics of what I consider good sex: the hunger, the curiosity, the eagerness, to surrender, to give into your needs, the satisfaction. ... This project is an open manifest to reclaiming what is given to all of us but what seems to be lost to the commercially driven. Owning 5 dildos is not proof of being sexually liberated. Knowing how and if you want to use them is.

"I make porn and I love it" —a collection of twelve vignettes— lives up to Murielle's goal of reclaiming the hunger, curiosity and surrender of pure sex. Ranging from one to ten minutes in length, they portray the sexual encounters and experiences of a total of twenty-nine attractive young women and men, including Murielle, who all "dare to share how they really experience their own sexuality." Reflecting Murielle's side gigs as a DJ as well as her trendy sense of sexy design, Murielle takes the erotic music video format yet a step further with a stylistically striking sound- and picture composition and creative editing. A rock-pop song that matches the action in both lyrics and melody accompanies each vignette. There is no dialog on any of the films, except for on two documentary designed short films.

The style varies from delicate to grunge. The cutting is attention grabbing in some of the films, in others seamless. Some of the films are shot in black and white, or with artistic filters; others in realistic color.

In content the sex ranges from soft to hardcore, embracing a plurality of moods and sexual experiences.

The opening vignette, "mon premier picnic" (my first picnic), featuring a sensual picnic in a meadow dark at night, is accompanied by a nostalgic melody; "she's about to lose it," sings a husky young male voice languorously to long slow guitar strokes. To the rhythm of the song we see the dimmed black-and-white images of two young women, naked except from their sexy delicate underwear, dancing, licking, circling each other in slow motion, smooth skin to skin, lips, tongues, whipped cream, wine, their long blond wavy hair clings to their dimples. The atmosphere is giddy, yet snug, their movements lingering and soft.

The second vignette, on the other hand, "take care of yourself," is driven by a quick almost impatiently happy pop melody. Presenting us first with a series of brief snapshots of a handful of people, women and men, in their private settings, we then get to see their individual sexual satisfaction in crosscuts, mostly as solo sex, the camera framing only their upper-bodies; the focus is on the expression of pleasure in their faces. Murielle is included in this vignette, receiving cunnilingus from her partner.

The soundtrack on the third vignette, "you're a woman i'm a machine," captures that hunger Murielle refers to in her manifesto. The opening picture frames the hands of a male athlete, white gloves, grabbing talcum from a tray, clapping his hands dry, ready for action. Charging the picture is the sound of a woman's heavy breathing. He jumps, reaching for the rings. Crosscut to a young couple in a simple bedroom; she's riding him, the camera focuses on her face and upper body. She's thin, with long straight hair, bangs, her breasts small, all of her blushing from her exertions and the pleasure. The camera crosscuts between her and the athlete throughout the vignette in impatient staccato cutting. She moans frantically towards the end.

The next vignette, "the inside is where it is at PART 1: le gas station" is a longer, ten-minute documentary about a couple who likes to have sex in public places, especially toilets. We see the two having sex in a series of public toilet stalls, the lighting harsh, the music hard. Between the sex numbers, Murielle interviews them about their fetish in the car on their way to the next toilet.

The premise of the five-minute "hand in glove" is simple: a beautiful young woman and man have sex, with foreplay, in their bedroom. The vignette is accompanied by another nostalgic rock song; "I love it when you come down," sings a hoarse male voice. Filmed in black-and-white with an almost constant use of images dissolving into one another, it captures the muted joy, passion and love the two share; they fit together, like hand in glove, their movements flowing effortlessly.

A loud but catchy rock song takes us down a highway late at night in "that certain need." The vignette has a dark, raw feel, communicated through the flickering unsteady shots of a man in jeans and T-shirt running down the highway with a truck behind him—a young woman is driving with another woman next to her. In the end he turns around and stops. The truck stops. He pulls off his T-shirt, and opens the door to the driver's seat. Leaning up against the door, pants pulled down and skirts up, the three have sex. It's crowded and dark, the pictures blurry.

The follow-up film "the inside is where it is PART 2: le cinema" portrays more sex in public places, but the esthetics in this one is less documentary and more artistic. The film begins with the two in an empty movie theater watching an old American instructional film, perhaps from the 40s, shot in black-and-white and with a man lecturing in voiceover on "what to do on a date." The burgundy red chairs in the dark theater give the picture a warm glow, at times soft filters are added too, or the film crosscuts to black-and-white shots with soft Hollywood lighting. At other times the shooting speeds up to fast motion, electronic house music, sometimes almost psychedelic.

The music on "actions/louder/words" on the other hand is calm. The film begins with a slow dance between a woman and a man kissing. She's blindfolded, her hands in his ruffled curls; dark soft curls surround her face. The picture is shot in black-and-white, but changes to color. A smaller picture of the two—him laying her down in bed and pulling up her black tank top—is pasted on top of this picture. In the next shot it fills the screen, then from another angle. Another picture from another angle where he teases a finger up inside her beneath her black cotton panties is overlaid on top of this one in a smaller frame. And in this way the film continues in an almost constant use of cutting with pictures added on top of each other, alternating from color to black-and-white to color. A woman begins to speak-sing along with the classical guitar being played. The insistent recitation of the woman, then by a man, both on top of each other, underscores the intensity in the quiet passion between the two. The explicit glimpses of cock and pussy in the midst of all the softness—skin, touch, bodies embracing, intertwined— give an almost circular effect. She rides him, he takes her. There is no beginning or end, "it turns and turns again," harmonizes the woman on the soundtrack.

The one-minute long "foolin'" is the shortest and probably sweetest vignette: a smiling nostalgic snapshot of a young couple. She laughs, her long straight hair dancing around her face, no French lingerie here, just simple cotton underwear; the two could be taken from a Gap commercial. It's all so loving, tender, and playful, the sound of children laughing on the circus parade-esque soundtrack; in the midst of it all, their bed collapses, laughter and applause ensue.

"le grand appetit" (the big appetite) is completely different: a piercing synthesizer music with a male voice spitting out his words brings us into a modernistic room with black and white leather furniture. Whereas the floating pictures in "foolin'" had a soft retro filter around them, this is filmed in rather glaring naturalistic real time. Even when the picture shifts from color to black-and-white, and the filming spins and speeds up, the impression is brutally naturalistic. This is also the only film that shows a middle-aged, less attractive character in the shape of a man, his body unfit, hair receding, his body language more aggressive, also in the way he pumps and at times spanks the women. The film portrays sex between two women and two men, their faces erased with blue marker as if to signalize something taboo. Otherwise the pictures are explicit, raw. The four pose for the camera and also photograph each other. There's a lot of pumping, jerking, fingering and partner exchange with the four heaped closely together. Still everything remains fairly hetero: the men stick to the women. This vignette also contains the DVD's only money shot where the middle-aged man stands up and sprays his sperm over the two women.

"j'ai rendez-vous avec vous" (i have a date with you)

also features group sex, but a happier kind, more life-affirming. The soundtrack, "Beats of Heart," is also playful. A young woman sings: "One two three, five six seven, me and my baby go to heaven. One two three, five six nine, me and my baby gonna have a good time. La la la, la la la, la la laaa." A girl and two boys are sitting in an intimate park gazebo, talking, laughing, one of the guys grins to the camera. In the next scene the three are in a jacuzzi, she between the two guys, kissing to her left and right, before they all move into a big bed. They make out, fool around, she gives one of them a handjob while she's being licked and fingered by the other. Then she has sex with each of the boys one at a time while the other's lying beside, watching, waiting. Smiles and laughter, sighs of pleasure.

The last film, "moodmidnight," features a rougher kind of lesbian sex than the first vignette, here between two tattooed voluptuous black haired women. But the picture is nostalgic in an almost yellowing black-and-white. And there's a romantic flair over the setting: the soft wallpaper, crocheted bed blanket, flowery bed headboard, and grand-motherly lamps on the mahogany night tables. The music is also at first mellow, and though it grows increasingly intense with a harder rock guitar playing, it keeps to a slow rhythm. Ominous notes are also introduced as the camera moves over instruments and sex-toys as their sex takes on more of a BDSM character with spanking, rough pumping, and deep fisting. But the atmosphere remains affectionate with laughter and smiles, and they conclude with tender kisses, before wiping themselves dry with tissues. In the concluding shots, the two take off their wigs and corsets, and leave the bedroom, the picture fading out.

Coco de Mer exquisite: Lushly styled erotic musical vignettes

Dutch-born Eva Midgley (b. 1967) from Amsterdam has gained a reputation across the world for her stunning erotic shorts that are of unusual beauty and composure. A multi-award-winning fashion director and filmmaker, her attention to detail and her sumptuous visual style combine to create works charged with emotion, beauty and elegance.

Eva started her career in advertising in Jakarta, Indonesia before she went on to direct fashion and beauty in her native country, including for *AD Magazine*. Eva returned to school in 2000 when she and her family moved to London. Here she took a series of intensive film courses at the National Film and Television School and at the Raindance Institute, which offers courses to filmmakers.[10] While studying, she wrote her first manuscript for a feature film (*Sandcastles*) and several short films, including experimental erotic ones.

At the nursery gates of a Montessori school in London where she was picking up her middle son, Eva met human rights activist and environmental campaigner Sam Roddick (b. 1971) who was picking up her two-year-old daughter. Sam, the daughter of Anita Roddick who founded the cosmetics company Body Shop—one of the first companies to prohibit the use of ingredients tested on animals, and to promote fair trade with third world countries—was at the time in the planning stages of Coco de Mer, a luxurious women oriented sex boutique which opened shortly afterwards in 2001 in Covent Garden. The two soon became friends. Recounts Eva: "We just got talking and spent hours at various school events talking about why it is that porn is effective? It's butt ugly. It offends. And yet, it gets you going in seconds."[11]

Sam invited Eva and her husband John, a fashion photographer, to shoot some pictures for Coco de Mer in conjunction with its opening, perhaps also do some filming of the photo shoot. This filming grew into its own project, which eventually turned into Eva's first ten-minute erotic short: *Honey and Bunny* (2004). Shot on 35 mm, the film is filled with exclusive underwear, sex toys, bondage props and furniture, all available for purchase from Coco de Mer, and here included in a sweet little kinky story about Honey and Bunny making a movie.

The mischievous retro silent film is introduced on crème colored background with credits written on the title card in the same elegant yet playful characters as those used on Coco de Mer's website: a black line drawn around the screen as a frame for the credits, a dollop of a wreath penciled in at each corner, a flower down to the left. The sound of birds chirping, bees buzzing: a butterfly flies over the screen and the text, more butterflies fly out of the flower.

The film's opening shot fades in from black background. In a 20s style drawing room, a flapper lady in a Charleston era dress, beige with black patterns, is hanging up long curtains over a window. Another flapper enters, looks into the camera; checks her hair.

Cut to the text frame: "One lovely afternoon in a place not far from you…"

The lady smiles into the camera, turns around, pulls out in fast motion a leather bench designed as a classy take on the gynecologist's chair (available at Coco de Mer as erotic furniture for around £5000, about $8000); lets her beige silk pantsuit fall to the floor, and poses for the camera. A sensual melody begins to play. She lies down on the bench, her gaze still on the camera, wiggling her legs in the air, high-heeled beige sandals on her feet. The flapper by the window turns to look at her, "Bunny, what are you doing?" She hurries to the camera, blocking the view.

Cut again to the text frame, the flower now resembling the two legs of a lady pointing up into the air, a butterfly escapes from her crotch, then more: "Honey and Bunny are making a movie."

In the next shot Bunny has put on another crème colored pantsuit and has also found a whip. She's sitting on the bench, testing it, her long brown curls and soft bangs dancing around her face. In the background a dark foreboding music: "It takes a special kind of person, to get you off." Bunny harmonizes the music: "Come on, come on Honey!" Enter Honey, with her feather-whip. She sits down on the bench's lower stool; Bunny in front of her up on the bench. The music escalates as the two ride the bench until Honey's had enough when Bunny accidentally whips her bum.

The text frame's illustration of the woman's legs is now replaced by a penis hopping around on the screen, ejaculating the word "Action!"

A languid woman's voice sings "you want me, honey, you want me" to a drawn out sexy rhythm. Honey cuts to action for the camera using two black wooden paddles as scene markers, and in comes Bunny; now in a black pantsuit. She sways her hips and lets the pantsuit fall down, revealing beige and black silk underwear. She unfolds the silk on top of one of her breasts; three cloth pieces reveal red fabric beneath, a naked breast in the middle. Then the other breast; she shakes her petite firm breasts.

Again the penis jumps around within the animated text frame, a couple of boobs in each corner now, the nipples erect: "Honey wants to liberate her breasts too!"

Honey is at this point wearing only black pumps and

black underwear, a big pink flower in her hair. She unveils her left boob by pulling on a string, a tickling music in the background.

Penis ejaculates a cloud of words on the text screen: "Honey knows a good game..."

Bunny gets a leather blindfold over her eyes; Honey finds a glass dildo. In the background a heavy alarming rock tune. Honey gives Bunny the dildo; she plays with it as a microphone, then as a part of a strap-on harness; the two dance with it slowly to the sound of the dark rhythms. Bunny bends over, shows Honey her bum; Honey teases the glass dildo between Bunny's buttocks before the text frame abruptly cuts their action:

"Let's play catch!"

A playful music now. Reclining in a chair, Bunny takes a bite of a little red apple before she laughingly tosses it; aimed at Honey's naked pussy in front of her on the floor. In slow motion she pitches a rain of red apples she's bitten into over Honey; we see Honey in profile sitting on the floor, interrupted by a swift close-up of an apple landing straight in her pussy, the open labia around it. The apple rolls to the side reveling a myriad of open spiraled pink and orange lips, a peach pussy.

"Oh!"

A slow rhythm introduces the next picture. Bunny gets down onto the floor on all four, lifts up an apple with her teeth, teases Honey's lips with it, lies down on top of her; the bodies of the two move out of the picture to the right; the last thing we see is one of Bunny's legs lifted up into the air flapper-style.

"The End."

The penis ejaculates the credits over the screen.

Honey and Bunny has won wide acclaim since its release. The film received an Honorable Best Mention at CineKink NYC (2006) and was a finalist at New York Festivals International Film & Video Awards.

After this success, Eva wrote and directed seven erotic vignettes for Coco de Mer: *Erotic Moments Collection* (2008). All of the seven vignettes (snippets from one to five minutes) are based on erotic fantasies collected by Coco de Mer. The vignettes' titles are: "Matryoshka" (an allusion to the Russian doll, the camera in this sensual vignette caresses the curves of a naked woman's body, a strawberry on top of her pussy, before freezing on her porcelain doll face — apparently, several customers reported fantasies about a woman with a strawberry pussy, and one also wrote that her face should be like that of a Russian doll);[12] "Footsie" (foot flirt between a foot and a penis); "Clean Laundry" (a playful spin on a typical porn cliché where a woman arrives in a basement laundry and has sex with the guy she finds hanging out there with his guitar); "French Maid" (a woman dressed as a French maid strips, for another woman, as it turns out; and for the first time — according to Eva, many straight women wrote that they fantasize about sex with another woman). Then there is "Heavy Petting" (where a young woman is stroking a goat, at peace out in nature, soft fur, warm sunshine on her face; she closes her eyes and enjoys, before looking straight into the camera. It's innocent, perhaps, but in this context troublingly close to bestiality). And "Pollinate" (the only animated vignette in this collection: a swarm of bees attack a woman who's sleeping in the shade of a tree, she writhes in pain, or pleasure?). And, finally "Drum Bum" (where a naked woman's buttocks replace an African drum).

In *Erotic Moments Collection* Eva's definite eye for esthetic detail is underscored in each shot, accompanied by a musical score that not only matches, but further lifts and moves the picture. The vignettes also reflect Eva's opposition to the clichés of mainstream porn and its clinical objectification of women's bodies, blind to the nuances and depths in the registry of women's and men's sexual desires and pleasure. Eva summarizes the vignettes as "little deliberations on sex, embracing the differences, bringing feeling and beauty back into sex."[13]

Most of Eva's "erotic moments" are, like *Honey and Bunny*, not particularly explicit, but several have been shown in conjunction with festivals for alternative porn in the United States and Europe, including Berlin Porn Film Festival. The vignettes were awarded a prize for Best Experimental Short Film at CineKink NYC in 2009.

"Clean Laundry" is the most "pornographic," but also the most amusing film; a playful twist on mainstream porn filmed in retro style with animated effects accompanied by a groovy rhythm and psychedelic jingles. Comments Eva about the fantasy on which this vignette is based:

> The laundry machine secret sexual fantasy stuck because I found it such a mundane fantasy. She (I am assuming she is a she, but don't actually know anything about the people who wrote it other than the fantasy/moment and their country of origin) wanted to do this with her boyfriend. What was stopping her? Why is this a secret sexual fantasy. Why not just get on that machine? She was from the Netherlands (like me). It made me wonder if all this sexual openness we've enjoyed has made us boring.[14]

While "Clean Laundry" is the most humorous of the short films, "Footsie" is the most lyrical and esthetically exquisite. "Footsie" was shown at the Institute of Contemporary Art in London in conjunction with the short film competition Destricted (2007), which it won. Destricted was a project initiated by a group of filmmakers including Larry Clark (known for his film *Kids*, 1995) and Gaspar Noé (who made *Irréversible*, 2002) to focus on the intersecting points of sex, art, and porn. Larry Clarke who chose the winners, said this about Eva's film:

"Eva Midgley is a fresh talent, I predict great things for her. ... ["Footsie" is] original, creative, erotic and really addresses the question where art and pornography meet."[15]

Interviewed about this film, which shows the foot flirt between a foot and a penis, Eva explains that she wanted to capture ejaculation in slow motion; she had heard about a special camera used in scientific research that is capable of shooting in just about any frame rate. I though it would be just "amazing" to see, she adds. And truly, it is.

Strictly choreographed, the camera frames only the man's penis and a woman's feet; naked skin in soft shades. The picture is accompanied by dramatic piano play. At first dark serious notes. Eventually light promising key strokes are blended in; slow and lingering, before dark strokes on a cello's strings are added. Then deeply vibrating violin notes; complexity and harmony. A soaring longing high pitch on top of all. The excitement mounts but the foot sex remains tender and intimate; the picture soft. As ecstasy impends, the film's tempo escalates in the shots' cutting and the movement of her feet, stroking his penis. The feet continue intently with their stroking movement in slow motion while the penis ejaculates for an entire minute and a half, the camera resting as the music lands. The picture resembles that of an athlete at the finish line captured in reruns, as if the penis were shaking out his sweat in a glistening glory around his head, spitting. The shimmering drops of sperm beaming out into space; a trickling fountain of sparkling drops that fall on the women's feet, the man's abdomen, and his hips.

In contrast to the lyrical quality of "Footsie," "Drum Bum" — illustrating spanking — is distinguished by its joyous celebration of life. According to Midgely, spanking was the most popular erotic experience reported, especially in the UK. And not as fantasy, but as experience. And usually as a sudden and surprising pleasure for a novice introduced to spanking by someone more experienced.[16]

"Drum Bum" features a naked woman's white bum and the hands of a black man merrily drumming away on it to a rhythmic African beat, cymbals added on eventually. While I had imagined being spanked in a sexual context for the first time would carry with it the deep undertones of unfamiliar depths and tensions, "Drum Bum" just has such a playful and light-hearted feel to it; when I watch it, I just want to dance! Perhaps this (also?) explains this short film's popularity? Or is it simply the case that this is how one feels after having been spanked sexually for the first time?

Before the release of *Erotic Moments Collection*, Eva had in 2005 moved to Brooklyn with her husband and their children. In 2009, she made the short film *Peep Show* (2009), a poetic narrative about a man who falls in love with a stripper, and who desperately tries to track her down and have her return to that job when she leaves to work as a waitress in a diner. And for Coco de Mer, she and her husband have made an almost painterly series of erotic photographs with dramatic light and dark contrasts. Her husband also served as director of photography for Eva's films. Explains Eva:

> I guess I still approach a lot of my film work the same way I approached my fashion work. The people I work with come from fashion, not film, so they all bring a certain different aesthetic and style with them, and a lot of attention to detail.[17]

Eva added this to me in an email:

> I am a subtle subversive. I rebel against the overload of bad porn, warped ideas of beauty in the fashion industry, and against music videos and commercials where so much is sold on the hidden promise of sex but god forbid you would ever see a nipple!
>
> This is why I have humor in the midst of a sex scene, dirty feet in a beauty piece, bees that are pleasuring a woman but wait are they really?

Concluded Eva:

> I'm communicating ideas and feminist opinions in a very lush package.[18]

Chapter 6

Cinematic Porn: Captivating Quality Films

The Band: Art house sex film from down under

Well-composed soundtracks also characterize the cinematic porn films we'll look at in this chapter, as they do for today's modern music video porn. But even when the music plays a highly central role, like in the art house sex and rock film *The Band* (shot in 2006 and finally released in 2009) by Australian Anna Brownfield (b. 1971), the films stand out even more so with their filmic ambitions, using film languages and styles as they push the boundaries of porn even further, eradicating the lines between cinematic-, art house-, sex film and porn. Tellingly, the year *The Band* was released it was the opening film at Berlin Porn Festival; it was also shown at Cannes Film Market, which is part of Cannes Film Festival. Anna's film is reminiscent of Michael Winterbottom's *9 songs* (2004) and John Cameron Mitchell's *Shortbus* (2006), films along with which Anna classifies her own; art house films with hardcore sex.[1]

Based in Melbourne—Australia's main seat for its television, film and music industry, and its second largest metropolis after Sydney—Anna has built recognition for herself as a competent filmmaker. She has a degree in Media Arts from the RMIT University with an emphasis on film and video production, and teaches courses in Film and Television at Swinburne University.

Anna founded Poison Apple Productions in the 90s, making a handful of experimental short films exploring women's sexuality. Her films soon received the attention of Australian media, with screenings at several festivals, both nationally and internationally. Among these earlier films is the lighthearted comedy *The Money Shot* (2002), a tongue-in-cheek commentary on the Australian porn industry.

To *Cleo* magazine, Anna explains that she started her company "after looking at pornography myself and finding nothing that appealed to me as a female."

> Most of it was geared toward the male heterosexual market — there was no sensuality or flirting, no kissing or build-up to the sex. I wanted to see something erotic that got me excited but didn't necessarily go straight into it.

Anna continues with a note on where she sees her work going:

> In my filmmaking I've always explored the theme of sexuality, in particular female sexuality, so moving into X-rated films seems like a normal progression. I want to make creative and interesting films — just because it's porn doesn't mean it has to be bad filmmaking.[2]

Four years later, having at this point shot her first sexually explicit feature film *The Band*, Anna further explains her views on porn as follows to *The Age* newspaper:

> There's nothing inherently sexist or degrading about porn, but I do have a problem with the most mainstream pornography because of the complete objectification of female bodies. My films are about breaking conventions. Running a finger up an arm can be just as sensual as anything else you might see, for example. And I also focus a lot more on the men. As a society, we're constantly exposed to the female form, yet we very rarely see male nudity or consider it to be attractive.[3]

True to her words, *The Band* does break conventions as it explores the diversities of male and female form and desire. And it is a cinematically sound film, driven by raw catchy punk-rock music and hardcore sex. The music was composed by the Melbourne-based band Moscow Schoolboy, with the PJ Harvey-esque vocalist Jess Cornelius. The acting is strong, with performers who fit their parts: believable punk-rock band members with their ups and downs.

Photography and cinematography are striking on this film, for which Anna gives director of photography Sanne Kurz much of the credit. The pictures are exceptional in the depth, layers, and textures that they convey, communicating excitement, heat, and passion, as well as affection and tenderness; all of which is further emphasized by the nuanced soundtrack that captures the sensations of licking and touching. Shot on a Panasonic AG-HVX200 camera with its variable shooting speed, the sex numbers are shot in true slow motion, which gives them a fluid quality.

In content the film pushes boundaries, portraying a range of sexual relations and experiences that include fetishes and gender bending encounters that are well integrated into the story. The film follows the rock group Gutter Filth on tour through clubs and rundown bars with their own groupie in tow. Bassist for the band is G.B. who looks like a younger version of Mick Jagger and who is constantly looking for a number but who is also equally happy on the receiving end. The band's drummer is Dee, a lean black-haired man with a fondness for women's attire and black eye makeup. And the band's manager is Jennifer, a caring and inconspicuously butch woman with dreadlocks and piercings.

> The vocalist and front figure for the band, the sexy but smug Jimmy Taranto, decides early on to give his solo career a shot and drops both the group and his girlfriend, Candy, a beautiful long-limbed and long-haired young woman who's too good for him anyway. Auditioning to be Gutter Filth's new vocalist, Candy impresses the band and secures the job. The record company wants to test the audience response to Gutter Filth's new front figure and sends the band on tour in the backblocks. The tour is successful and the band's new single with Candy reaches number one on the top hit list, while Jimmy's popularity plummets to the bottom.

Anna won the award for Hottest Feature Film at the Feminist Porn Awards in 2010 and signed a contract with Breaking Glass Pictures to distribute her indie sex and rock film in the United States and Canada. The film now also has distribution in Germany, France, and Korea, but still not in Australia. This is not really surprising, considering Australia's strict regulation of explicit films and porn, as we've seen. Anna is currently writing a new erotic film titled *Screwed in Suburbia*, for which she has already secured a US distributor who have indicated they might also take on the international distribution of the film.

Blue Artichoke Films: Textural feeling

Blue Artichoke Films in Amsterdam is also making a name for itself by producing cinematic quality porn. US-born Jennifer Lyon Bell (b. 1969) is the creative force behind its films, which are of notable atmosphere and textural feel. As Jennifer puts it, Blue Artichoke Films offers "erotic films for people who like film" made by "a small group of film enthusiasts dedicated to making artistic, unusual erotic films that portray sexuality in an emotionally realistic way."[4]

Jennifer grew up in Boston and has a Bachelor's in psychology from Harvard where she also studied film theory. Jennifer's family moved to the San Francisco Bay area when she was eleven. Her parents had nurtured an open attitude to sexuality, she explains to Dutch television, and on the west coast she found people in general being more relaxed about sex.[5] She moved to Amsterdam in 1999, completed a Master's in film studies at the University of Amsterdam in 2001, and then launched her company Blue Artichoke Films in 2004.

Jennifer recounts pondering all the way back in high school how porn could be changed to appeal to women. She says she thinks that for women, getting to know the characters they see is important, as well as the lead-up to their sex, the context and story behind it. She also points out the importance of stylistic quality — the textures. Including hairstyles that look nice, and make-up that you believe a woman would wear. She adds that she *does* think women like to see explicit sex too. That it's not like they can't handle it. But that explicit can be nicer![6]

Jennifer's first film, however, does not show any explicit sex; yet its sexiness rises up into the frame from what the viewer doesn't actually see. A ten-minute short, *Headshot* (2006) literally shows a man from his shoulders up — as he's getting a blowjob. As Jennifer explains, the point with this film is to show how it can be erotic not so much because of *what* you see, but because of what you *do not* see.

We hear a woman enter through a door, and the man briefly speaks with her before she kneels down in front of him. We only catch a glimpse of the back of her head. Then there's the sound of her sucking and pumping. But first and foremost the man's face is in full view and speaks to the viewer: the shivering contractions of his features, the expression in his eyes, his breath, moans, sighs; how his face shuts and opens when he comes, his big charming smiles afterward, and the look of *wow!* that he radiates.

Headshot screened at Cannes Short Film Corner in 2006, and at the Institute of Contemporary Art in London in 2007 in conjunction with the above-mentioned Destricted project. *Headshot* won the award for Best Short Erotic Film at the Atlanta Underground Film Festival (2009).

Jennifer's first explicit sex film, the half-hour long film *Matinée* (2009), reflects Jennifer's views on porn and feminism. This is how she explains them at Blue Artichoke Films online:

Jennifer's mission to create better sex film is an integral part of her feminist sexual expression. She believes that sexual freedom is an essential component of women's freedom. And that creating beautiful, hot films that turn women on is possible, safe, and necessary.

We're certainly not anti-porn; on the contrary, we think there should be much more good porn available!

Part of our appeal to modern women is that our stories and situations aren't bound up in monogamous romance. Pop culture is rife with messages for women that sex is only awesome once they've found True Love. Love is lovely, but we think that hot, meaningful sex can also happen between total strangers.

There's one thing that sexfilm made for men consistently fails to give straight women, and that's footage of good-looking men. So we look for actors who are engaging, cute, and interesting-looking, and when we edit the film, we make sure you really get to know the male characters too — on the outside and the inside.

Lastly, it's of the utmost concern to us that the actors and (particularly) actresses we work with be knowledgeable, thoughtful, and enthusiastic about doing films with us. Jennifer meets personally with every actor and actress even before allowing them to audition, so that she can be sure they have like-minded motivations and understand what the risks might be. Also, everyone on the cast and crew is encouraged to ask questions. We think that's the only way to create a safe space for people to experiment sexually.[7]

Presented as "a fresh look at what erotic film can be ... [an] erotic film for people who like film," *Matinée* is about Mariah and Daniel, two theater actors who perform the parts of lovers: Lola and Tony in the play *Two Days in Berlin*. Despite a sense of personal chemistry between the two, we learn that reviews of the play have critiqued their performance for lacking spark.

Jennifer explains that for *Matinée* she wanted a story to develop the main characters and the intensely emotional sex the two have. But not necessarily a romantic story. She didn't want her film to fall into the clichés about women wanting roses, champagne, and romance. She wanted to create feminist porn where the female character is also in control — and where the male character doesn't drop his underwear right away...[8]

During a pre-play rehearsal at the beginning of the film, Daniel suggests to Mariah that they improvise in a significant reunion scene to make it more natural. A New York talent agent will be in the audience, meaning this could be a big break for either if the performance goes well; that it could serve their art. Mariah is skeptical at first, but later decides to give it a go — placing a condom in the pocket of the kimono that she will be wearing during this scene before entering the stage. The set is stark with black curtains and only a bed with dark gray sheets in the middle of the stage.

The camera scans the audience and establishes this viewing perspective. We see "Lola" reading in bed. Then "Tony" enters. Neither fits a popularized ideal of beauty, but both are attractive in their anachronistic ways. She's plumper, pale skin and blond dreadlocks gathered in a loose ponytail, a furrow between her eyebrows, some thin lines along her neck, full lips and eyes to sink into. He's thin, short coarse dark hair, a distinct jaw, fine lines around his mouth and eyes, his gaze present. I didn't think you'd come, she says.

Daniel walks over to Mariah. She gets up to receive him, running her hands through his hair. After looking into his eyes for an extended moment, she kisses him and lightly glides her hand over his shoulder and back. They embrace. With a pleasure-filled smile, she kisses him more passionately. They pause to check in, each looking once again into the eyes of the other; he gives a subtle, knowing expression. She guides his hand under her kimono onto her naked breast.

We see a close-up of the talent agent, and then another shot of the stage through the audience from her perspective. The theater is completely still. And then Mariah slides off her kimono and drops it on the bed.

Before continuing, both Mariah and Daniel cast glances out over the audience. At first he is following her lead, but soon they begin to take cues from each other. They touch and caress each other gently, and look intimately at each other. All this time, however, the intimacy of their experience is heightened by their exposure to watchful eyes; occasional shots show audience members being drawn into the scene through the invisible fourth wall, as the performance touches them in new ways.

Squeezing his hand, Mariah sits down in bed; he follows her lead and sits down too, taking off his shoes while she holds him, stroking and kissing him. He lays a hand on her thigh; she guides it up to her crotch, leaves it there. The assistant in the wings gasps. Daniel closes his eyes as he begins to stroke her vulva. Mariah lies down, gets him down with and over her, sliding her fingers down his belly.

As he kisses and nibbles her breast, she reaches down for his crotch and begins to rub him there; we can hear the almost scratchy sound of her hand against the fabric of his pants. He rubs his body towards her naked body. We hear the sound of his belt and zipper being opened. Their breathing hectic, they kiss, the camera spinning around them, their arms and legs. He gets up just enough to get his pants off, then lies down again, still in his underwear. He begins to finger her gently while moving his face slowly down her belly kissing it. With his gaze fixed on her face, he begins to kiss her between her thighs, on her vulva. "Gently," she whispers between her sighs and heavy breathing, holding on to the headboard rails.

He fingers her again, she strokes his penis; together they get his underwear off, his erect penis lifts up towards her. To the sound of the two kissing, breathing, and sighing, the camera glides over the audience, following the action intently. She strokes him again; he fingers her, faster, more and more intensely.

Then she pauses to reach for the condom in the kimono, as improvising takes on new meaning. Mariah takes a deep breath, and looks at him; will you do this with me? Daniel gives a questioning look, himself not sure; do you want to do this? She nods, with the hint of a smile on her lips. Each searches deeply into the eyes of the other.

She opens the pouch, pulls the condom on him, looks at him with big eyes. Then she sucks him. His forehead contracts in pleasure. Ready, she lies down on her back again, and with an arm around his neck, she gets him down with her. Leading his penis inside of her, we see him enter from her perspective as she looks down her belly. Then a close-up of Daniel penetrating her from behind, captured between his legs, his body rocking back and forth, gently at first.

The shifting of positions seamless, their movements floating from one to the next, she sits up on top of him, and guides his penis inside of her with her hand. Riding him, she moans loudly. The camera spins around them. She pumps him while fingering herself, quickly, her buttocks smacking against his balls. A young woman in the audience looks at her boyfriend, her hand on his thigh. The agent still watches intently, resting her chin in her hand. Mariah lies down next to Daniel and asks him to "do it again." And he fingers her again while she rocks her hips, her head on his arm and her hand in his. Closing her eyes in pleasure, she comes this way while he fingers her, her face contracting in ecstasy. Mariah sighing out, the agent smiles to herself, pleased.

Then with close-ups of bodies meshed, the two roll over together; the shivering contractions in his features as he comes, and a few last sighs of pleasure from her as she shares his ecstasy, her nails digging into the flesh of his back.

Both sighing out, they embrace each other, holding one another in a loving gaze. I don't know what to say, "Lola" says and we recognize the line from their rehearsal. Just say that I can stay, "Tony" replies. She kisses him softly. We see them on the bed from the perspective of the talent agent one last time, as the stage lights dim and all goes black.

In the next scene Mariah is in her wardrobe. She has the kimono on again and is adjusting her make-up as Daniel knocks on her door. What happened out there, he asks, a smile in his voice. "We were finally serving our art," she replies simply, referencing a point he made during their rehearsal discussion. He grins, "good answer!" The assistant comes by, "ten minutes till final curtain, and I have a note for Daniel." It's from the agent; she wants to meet after the performance. With both of them. Mariah raises an eyebrow, happy and excited; he is the most famous of the two. "Good show," he nods to her on his way out, she smiles proudly. In the film's final shot she's beaming to herself in the mirror as the music of a victorious beat lifts her up even higher.

Matinée is a unique viewing experience. Jennifer focuses on natural beauty and chemistry between the two characters, with close-ups that capture the warmth and textures of skin and curves, filming the sex in near real time accompanied solely by the sensual sounds of sex. As bookends the film features an effective original music score, but more noticeable during the sex scene is the resounding stillness of the theater through which the real sounds of each touch truly add to the atmosphere of the film—as if the viewer can feel the tingle of this kind of sexuality.

The narrative framework of it taking place in the theater in front of an audience is well integrated and adds to the overall texture of the picture, so that the filling of the theater space with these sounds helps to enliven the senses. In whole, the film bears testimony to Jennifer's commitment to delivering cinematic quality. *Matinée* won the awards for best short film at Melbourne Underground Film Festival (2009) and at CineKink NYC (2009), and also received an Honorable Mention at the Feminist Porn Awards (2009).

Skin. Like. Sun. (2009; original title is *Des Jours Plus Belles Que La Nuit*) is Jennifer's third film, which she collaborated on with Murielle Scherre. Also filmed in near real time, *Skin. Like. Sun.* is an art house style sex film that lingers on the sweet and sexy slowness of sex. Stylistically, the film combines the strength of each filmmaker: the cinematic realism and fine eye for close-ups with texture of Jennifer and the indie rhythm and esthetics of D.J. and lingerie designer Murielle.

The film follows a real-life couple spending an afternoon having sex in the sun-washed rooms of an empty old house (the couple is also featured in Murielle's documentary styled shorts on *J'fais du porno et j'aime ça*). Far from porny looking, the woman and man are attractive in their indie, tattooed, subtly sexy and emotionally naked way. And their mutual affection and chemistry emanate from the picture.

Originally the filmmakers' idea was to capture how sex looks like from her perspective, but in the end they realized that would detract from also capturing what she feels. And the film well captures his deeply felt adore for her in his eyes and caresses.

At about 55 minutes in length, the film is unique too for its focus on foreplay. It also captures that dizzying bubble of pleasure as the intensity soars and the couple lose themselves to the moment. The pulsing rhythms of the almost metallic sounding soundtrack before the intimate sounds of the couple's breaths and sex take over, surrounded by a nostalgic lyrics sung by a raspy male voice and insistent guitar strokes, work well to further develop the atmosphere.

There are no distinct episodes on *Skin. Like. Sun.*, but bridging the sex that the couple have is an interlude with a distinctly different feel from the rest of the film, dividing the film into two sections. After exploring the house, the couple make slow and sweet love in the main room on the wooden floor. They get dressed while talking softly and then move into another room with sheepskins on the floor. An almost sinister but also upbeat rhythm sets in as the couple begin to fool around again. And whereas the first part reflects more of Jennifer's eye for close-ups with texture, this second part signals Murielle's penchant for creating textures through a creative mixture of techniques, combining spinning camera movements and dissolving images that bleed in and out of each other, the reflection of the sun in the lens, the picture blurry.

Then they giddily move on: up the stairs, through rooms and hallways, teasingly and playfully chasing each other around. They end up in the bathroom where they have sex again, leaning up against the wall, then seated on the toilet, then again against the wall. She comes, then he. And again they come to, they smile and talk quietly, giggly, and wipe themselves off with toilet paper before he lovingly helps rinse off her legs in the bathtub.

Skin. Like. Sun. was made upon invitation by the Belgian feminist festival Stout(ste) Dromen [Your Wild(est) Dreams] in Antwerp where it premiered in October 2009. The film had its international premiere during CineKink NYC in February 2010. Included as extra material on the DVD are interviews with the filmmakers and the performers sharing their views on feminism and what makes *Skin. Like. Sun.* a feminist film, in particular in how it captures mutual love and respect, and in how it focuses on her experience and what real unscripted sex is like for her, and for him. (The couple make sure to point out that it's not like their sex is always this slow and sweet; that they sometimes like it rough too! But that sweetness fit "the vibe of the moment" in a beautiful and relaxed sunlit space.)

The couple also stress that having sex this intimately before a camera became possible for them only because of the connection they felt with Murielle and Jennifer; a fundamental sense of trust and respect that allowed the couple to relax and feel free to just be like themselves. And they talk about what taking part in the film has meant to them, including the gift of seeing the beauty of their sex on film and how they now feel even more free and natural in their sex life. She also mentions becoming more sure about her body, and how the removed perspective of watching the film on television highlighted how sweetly he actually looks at and touches her when they have sex. How you learn more and get deeper into each other.

Skin. Like. Sun. won the award for Best Direction at the Feminist Porn Awards (2010).

Jennifer has several projects in development, including a trilogy featuring three parallel stories of erotic urgency that unfold in the same apartment, an art film with explicit sexuality set specifically in Amsterdam, and an erotic documentary following the conflicting emotions of a feminist exploring the different facets of BDSM. She also curates film festivals and cultural events and leads workshops on topics that pertain to sex and film.

Très chic X-femmes: Upscale designed shorts

France has a long tradition of artists challenging our conception of sexuality in often disturbing ways. Think only of Marquis de Sade or Georges Bataille, and today also a growing number of female artists including Catherine Breillat and Virginie Despentes. Opposing the disturbing portrayal of sex and violence in these highbrow artists' work, Ovidie (b. 1980) received a lot of attention from the media when she entered the porn scene only eighteen years old as a brooding goth philosophy student with short black hair, eyes painted black, her pale skin tattooed and pierced. A militant left-wing sex-positive feminist, she was nicknamed "L'intello du porno" ("porn-star intellectual") and became a popular guest at radio and television talk shows, captivating audiences with her charm and level-headed intellect.[9]

Interviewed by *The Guardian*, Ovidie explains why she got involved in the making of porn, first through acting, then also by directing:

> Why did I decide to act in these movies? I began to think that feminism and pornography might not be incompatible after all. Since feminists' battleground is sexuality, they have to become involved in its representation — and therefore in pornographic movies. All these new ideas led me into a world where these women whom I had once pitied now seemed admirable and impressive. I wanted to have an equally powerful sexual image.
>
> The other reason was my fascination with the body, as a keen amateur dancer and choreographer interested in the whole area of movement. I see a pornographic scene as a piece of choreography that involves the whole body, in which one must show the emotions by moving, by tensing one's muscles, by trembling and by letting go. It's a very interesting exercise in physical expression.

Why did I become a director? I simply wanted to put on screen my imagination and my feminist aspirations. I wanted to make films where the emotional dimension and sexual practices would be totally different in each pornographic sequence — something I only achieved with my second film, *Lilith*.[10]

Ovidie started directing only a year after she began acting. Approached by the French high gloss producer Marc Dorcel, she first made *Orgie en noir* (2000), a gothic concoction that reflects Dorcel's style. And then in 2001, Dorcel produced Ovidie's feature film *Lilith*. The opening scene introduces us to Lilith; a young woman left dissatisfied with her boyfriend's lack of attention to her sexual needs. The remainder of the film follows Lilith after she's left her boyfriend to pursue her own sexual journey to find satisfaction for her unmet desires.

In 2002, Ovidie's book *Porno Manifesto* (in French) was published. Here Ovidie makes the argument that good porn is the mark of a stable and healthy society. She continued to direct and act in porn, including in the Puzzy Power film *All About Anna* where she plays the role of the French theater actress Sophie. But gradually and especially after she became a mom, her focus shifted towards sex education, writing sexuality guides and directing sexological films. Most recently, she took the helm of the production department of a pay-for-view adult sex education and inspiration television channel French Lover TV, which was launched in 2009. Drawing "on the inspiration of everyday life for creating its programs,"[11] French Lover TV also set out to produce films featuring "real sex" that would "reduc[e] the gap between porn movies and your reality."[12] The first of these films is *Histoires de sexe(s)* (2009), co-written and co-directed by Ovidie and Jack Tyler, with the concept of having the perspectives of both sexes included in the film's making.

An interesting concept and a good conversation starter for couples, *Histoires de sexe(s)* (in French with English subtitles) addresses realistic relationship issues among couples, and portrays how differently the women and men describe and experience their sex lives. The film crosscuts between a group of female friends—mostly in their twenties and thirties, some are moms—gathered one evening over food, drink, and talk, and the men hanging out in another apartment for the same purpose. Relationship issues and sex are recurring topics of both conversations. Interspersed throughout are clips of the sex the women and men talk about, some of which are shot twice to provide both the male and the female perspective. The clips reveal striking differences in the perceptions of sex that the women's and men's separate conversations further underscore.

The film's featured characters are modern, urban, and (mostly) sophisticated women and men (the inclusion of a conventional dude and a more reserved woman adds dynamic to their discussions). The acting is strong and the sex scenes flow well within the story. The style is very French chic and attractive, the picture quality polished.

Histoires de sexe(s) was shown at Berlin Porn Film Festival (2009) where Ovidie participated on a panel titled "Chicks with Guts," discussing with other new female porn producers how sex, porn, feminism, female self-confidence, new gender identities, and cliché-breaking experiments in film go together.[13]

* * *

Today, Paris has become one of the most important centers for new progressive sex films made by intellectual women with high artistic ambitions. They are fronted by Sophie Bramly (b. 1959) who had originally built a successful career for herself in the music industry, first in the United States and then in Europe where she was part of the team that launched MTV Europe. But at one point, Sophie decided to leave her position at Universal Music and start her own company. Her intent was to produce quality sexual material aimed at women. It was her then six-year-old daughter who spurred Sophie's decision. One day, she had asked Sophie about the media's representation of women, which caused Sophie to pause for a moment. And then in 2007, she launched SecondSexe.com, an online magazine devoted to women's sexual pleasures. Its name a tribute to Simone de Beauvoir's classic feminist work *The Second Sex*, the website has an elegant intellectual upper class feel.

Sophie also established SoFilles Productions and solicited the interest of other women working in film and entertainment about making erotic short films with a focus on women's sexuality for her company. The result is *X-femmes* (2008), a collection of six short films, followed by *X-femmes 2* (2009), which includes four short films. Currently, Sophie is working on two feature films, one of them for theatrical release.

Since the Canal Plus premiere of the first X-femmes film at the Max Linder Panorama movie theater in Paris in September 2008, the films have been shown at several film festivals, nationally and internationally, including at the short film festival Circuito Off in Venice (2008, 2009). The French satellite television channel Canal Plus has played the short films over two seasons.

In an early press release, SoFilles Productions associates their X-femmes films with the recent trend in mainstream cinema to portray sex more explicitly, and in particular in films by female directors such as Jane Campion among others who are seeking to portray women's sexuality more truthfully.[14] According to SoFilles Productions, the X-femmes films achieve what these other films do not because of the rating system to which the directors of those films have to adhere.

Simply put, the X-femmes films are all très chic, testimony to the talented women who made them. The cinematic production value is high, the editing slick. All the actors are very attractive, dressed in stylish designer costumes. And their acting is strong. The films feature cosmopolitan Parisian sets and locations. And true to Sophie's background in music, the sexy soundtrack on every film complements the story well.

The goal of SoFilles Productions has been to produce films "that would let women see themselves as they are," explains Sophie in an interview with *The Guardian*. "Most women don't recognize themselves in porn films — they're too vulgar." Sophie therefore doesn't want to call her films "porn." They are explicit, she explains, but "I don't call them pornographic because pornography belongs to men."[15] In another interview, Sophie talks about all the pressures facing today's modern women; how we're supposed to be successful in so many areas, with respect to our careers, our families, our looks. How women get too tired to have sex and how can we change that. How women need to become more informed and aware of their sexuality; and encouraged and inspired to claim and own it.[16] To *The New York Times*, Sophie stresses her wish to empower women: "They work incredibly hard and they wake up one day to find that the husband has run off with a younger woman who usually looks just like the one he married in the first place. We're telling women, 'Get some pleasure.'"[17]

True to this sentiment, the SoFilles Productions' X-femmes films present the viewer with inspiring role models: modern competent women who in tune with their sexuality, act on their desires. In the twenty-minute film "Pour Elle" (2009; For Her), for instance, which was written and directed by the Spanish choreographer and ballet dancer Blanca Li (b. 1964), a happily married mature businesswoman secures the fulfillment of a longtime erotic fantasy—to have sex with another man—as a gift from her husband. Performing the part of the businesswoman is the unparalleled Victoria Abril (b. 1959) who has starred in several films by the Cannes and Oscar awarded film director Pedro Almodóvar.

In the film's opening scene, we see the sparkling petite brunette Abril onboard a train, barely escaping a collision with a handsome younger man in the crowded area by the toilet. A momentary flirt as the two exchange apologies continues in silence after she's returned to her seat, opposite his a few rows down. They exchange looks; she discreetly bares a leg.

Her husband awaits her at the station, a sophisticated man with a friendly face, a touch of gray in his hair. She kisses him, whispers something in his ear; casts a glance in the direction of the man from the train. Her husband nods, devotedly, an affectionate smile on his lips. She hurries on alone in high-heeled beige pumps while her husband catches up with the younger man, convinces him to join him for coffee at a coffee shop. Explains to him there how he's finally decided to grant his wife her erotic fantasy; he wants to give it to her as a gift. She's given him so much, more than he could ever wish for, he doesn't want to lose her, knows it has nothing to do with him, that it won't affect their relationship. The man's first reaction is disbelief. He gets up to leave; the husband holds him back, stressing again that this really is truly for *her*, what *she* desires, nothing kinky, not a threesome with him as well. The man's skepticism is eventually eased and in the end he agrees. And then he did appear attracted to her on the train too. Her husband follows him to their apartment, unlocks the door for him and, before leaving, insists he be good to his wife.

The apartment is luxurious. She has poured herself a glass of white wine and is reviewing some documents. She looks up from her reading glasses as he enters, gets up and walks towards him with anticipation in her eyes. He kisses her before she gets the chance to say anything, and they kiss, first tenderly, then passionately, pausing to look each other in the eye. Then they tumble into the living room; she falls down on the sofa. He undresses her slowly; she's fit with small firm breasts. He kisses her all over. Then she him, licking his naked muscular chest; feels his hard penis inside his pants, pulls them off. The playful melody we first heard on the train sets in again and follows their sex from here on.

Everything about the picture is exquisite; their bodies, the settings, even the condom that is teased on, close-ups of her riding him, in the foreground two glasses of white wine. He rides her from behind while making small circles with his firm butt and hips; then she rides him again while he firmly applies his hands on her clitoris. She reaches ecstatic levels, grasps a pillow, bangs it excitedly in his face, comes! "What's your name?" she asks him as she lands. He answers by turning her over, taking her from behind, from the side, she on top of him again facing away from him, her eyes fixed on a framed photograph of herself and her husband. The camera spins around skin, intertwined bodies, his hand lightly spanking her bum, her face writhing in ecstasy; and she comes again. "Merci, mon amour!" she exclaims to the photograph.

A woman's suggestion to role-play with her partner is the premise of "Samedi Soir" (2009; Saturday Night) by the American director Zoé R. Cassevetes (b. 1970). Zoé is best known for *Broken English* (2007), an independent movie about a female New Yorker's search for love in Paris. *Broken English* was nominated for numerous awards, including at Sundance Film Festival. It won Best First Film at Philadelphia Film Festival (2007).

In the opening scene of "Samedi Soir," the lead couple is at a dinner party at some friends, a group of attractive women and men in their early thirties. After eating, the friends linger at the table around plates and trays with leftovers of cheese and grapes, empty wine bottles; many are smoking. A tad tipsy, the hostess grumbles about how her husband doesn't see her as a woman anymore; just as a mother. How he's always working. The lead woman rolls her eyes to her boyfriend. When the host leaves the room to get more wine, the two sneak off with him to sniff cocaine in the pantry. The host apologizes for his wife: she's with the kids so much, she's had it; you need to be there to get that.

Back home in the couple's loft apartment, they sniff more cocaine, she lights candles, pour drinks. They kiss; undress. A psychedelic music illustrates their intoxication. The camera spins between chaotic close-ups of body parts, skin, curves. He takes her from behind, anally too is the suggestion. Dark tones, moans and dissonance in the soundtrack.

Afterwards they smoke pot, talk. He's trimmed his pubic hair and she teases him for his Brazilian stripe; she likes her pussy hairy. She gets up to pee, and shivering from a chill, she puts his jacket on. "Don't wipe," he whispers after her; he's put on her pink silk underwear. Whistling a tune as she pees, she looks at herself in the mirror, long blond curly hair around her face. She puts her hair up, calls out; "Mathieu, I've got an idea."

In the next scene Mathieu has put jeans and a coat on over the pink underwear, walks down and out into the street and heads over to a sex shop. Crosscut to her back in the apartment, sniffing more cocaine. She draws a mustache above her lips. Then puts on the pants that go with the jacket. When Mathieu returns, a note greets him: "put this on and meet me in the bedroom." She has set out a pink wig, black dress, and high heels for him.

He sniffs some more cocaine before joining her; psychedelic tunes lurk in the background. She kisses him, lies down on her back in bed, and gets him to undress her pants and jacket; she keeps the tie loose around her neck. Then she helps him up in bed and down over her. Pulls off the dress and tells him to turn over, onto all four. She gets up to put on what he's bought: strap-on equipment. The rhythm picks up with dark notes mounting as she adjusts the harness, finds a condom for the dildo. Then she penetrates him. He's nervous; "you're hurting me!" He pulls away, she holds him back; "c'mon, it's ok!" He tells her she's being too hard. "You go at it hard, too," she retorts. "Trust me, I'll be gentle," she pleads. He complies, likes it too; she pumps him while circling her hips. He turns over onto his back; she rides him. Comes! And she lands while lying next to him, the dildo erect into the air. Gazing out of the window, she mumbles to him; "it's either early or late," but he's already asleep. She kisses him, turns off the light, and snuggles next to him.

A young woman's desire to see her husband strip for her on her birthday—at a kinky sex club in full view of all its clients—is the premise of "Peep Show Heroes" (2008) by the Belgian artist Helena Noguerra (b. 1969). More explicit in content, the film also stands apart with its underground style as opposed to the luxuriously sophisticated touch of "Pour Elle" and the grungy bohemian edge of "Samedi Soir." A constant use of filters creates a retro effect in "Peep Show Heroes," while the frequent splitting of the screen image into two, three or more gives the feel of an ultra modern music video. The cutting is extremely fast, the camera angles striking, the costumes outrageous in their cutouts, nylon colors, and latex.

The film begins in full speed at night in a Cadillac cruising down a highway to an upbeat music. The dark night imbued with a bluish pink tint with shimmering streetlamps along the road, the scene has the feel of a dance club. Driving is a young woman dressed in a tight fitting blue latex suit with matching blue latex mask pulled down her face, covering her head and hair like a bathing cap. Sitting next to her is her boyfriend dressed in a dark suit, a red blindfold over his eyes. In voiceover the woman tells us in English that she is "Supergirl" and she is driving because her boyfriend "Wonderboy" is for the moment blind. "It's my birthday today, I'm twenty-one. I just want to have fun. Come!" she invites us.

In frantic tempo we're taken along into the night, fast motion through spiraling orange tunnels, arriving downtown and its chaotic traffic late at night, cars honking. A retro road trip melody starts to play as bright garish signs fly by announcing various lounges, clubs, sex clubs. Supergirl stops at one of them; guides her boyfriend down a narrow stairway, brick walls. A vaudeville chocolate sales girl with a black mustache drawn above her lips meets them in the reception before they are led through the club's hallways, in slow motion as if under-water to the packed sound of bubbles, fast heartbeats. Other customers in kinky masks and costumes are guided into their separate booths. Supergirl and Wonderboy stop by a red curtain; she removes his blindfold, revealing a black painted band over his eyes; "go on my darling," she bids him.

And off he goes. Through the curtain, down a spiral stairway that leads him to an elevated circular stage with a pole in the middle, shimmering curtains along the red walls. A small window is unveiled, behind it a woman in short sparkling blue and red disco gear watches him. He looks around, gets it, smiles a little. When a burlesque striptease melody with a charming rhythm begins to play—"lazy, you say I'm lazy," sings a woman languidly—he begins to strip. From here on the camera crosscuts constantly between him and those looking at him through the windows of their separate stalls around the stage. Many of them are women; one of them, Miss Disco, has shimmering stardust—turquoise, gold, and brown—all over her body. Another is dressed in glittering red with a red hooded mask. A man is dressed as Spiderman. Supergirl finds her own stall, leans back in the chair. The music is muffled behind the windows looking out on the stage, creating a charged atmosphere.

Wonderboy is in the groove, rocking his hips, dropping one piece of clothing after the other until he's down to a pair of green tight fitting boxer shorts. At one point "Cowboy" joins him on the stage, wearing cowboy boots and a cowboy hat, cut-off denim shorts and a plaid shirt. Wonderboy makes room for him and Cowboy continues to strip with a content grin on his face. Supergirl teases a hand under her blouse, strokes her breast. The picture is split from one to two, then three pictures that fill the screen. In one she has a hand on her breast, in the second a hand on her pussy; in the third and biggest picture, she has a leg lifted up, pressing against the wall, revealing long bronze boots that reach her all the way up to her hips. The screen fades to black before a picture of her getting up from her chair flashes in on the screen at the top left. In a larger picture to the right, we see her gliding down the pole to meet the guys. A third picture shows a beglittered young woman masturbating in her stall.

Supergirl and the two men fill the screen; her suit has cutout openings for her breasts and her pussy. The men are naked now; Cowboy licks and fingers her, we hear the sound of her juices and muffled moans. Wonderboy is stroking his cock next to them, then she strokes it; Miss Disco is stroking her breasts and pussy.

The curtains to Spiderman's closet close, interrupting his masturbation: "quick, quick, a token!" When the curtains unveil his window, the screen is filled with a picture of Supergirl, Wonderboy and Cowboy lying together on the elevated stage before splitting into more shots and close-ups. A frantic synthesizer rhythm has replaced the burlesque striptease song.

The curtains close again; Spiderman adds more tokens. The lady in blue and red disco gear has just about removed all her clothes entirely, masturbating intensely, captured in double red filtered shots.

Supergirl is also naked now; abundant long platinum

blond hair flows around her face, her eye make-up heavy. The film escalates through ultra quick cutting between a series of filtered estheticized shots of the three engaging in hardcore sex; the screen fractured into a labyrinth of sex and kink in form and shape, gloss and glitter. In filtered close-ups we see the face of a women coming; her features contract, the picture doubled up. In the final shot, Supergirl is riding her boyfriend with her back facing him; she comes, her face shimmering from sweat. In slow motion the camera rests on her from her hips up. *"FIN."*

The prize-awarded French actress Melanie Laurent (b. 1983) takes us through a more discreet sex club in her film "A Ses Pieds" (2008; At Her Feet). Its style more muted with an almost nostalgic feel, this film features a woman subtly seducing a stranger and finding her own kind of pleasure from a distance before leaving the man behind.

The film begins with a poised dark young woman languidly dressing in long black stockings, high heels, red corset and underwear, and an elegant beige coat dress that she folds about her with a black belt around her waist. She has a sheer veil over one of her eyes, and soft curls around her face.

She walks to a dimly lit bar, empty except for the bartender and one customer: a young attractive man in jeans and brown leather jacket. She sits down on a stool a couple chairs away, orders a glass of white wine, and lights up a cigarette in a mouthpiece. She casts the man a lingering look. Then she gets up to leave, having barely touched her wine; her cigarette is still burning on the ashtray. Passing him, she pauses; turns to look at him again, but says nothing.

He quickly pays and walks after her. Hurries down some stairs that lead him to an old-fashioned hotel with long dimmed corridors and stairways, candles burning on the floor along the railings, leading the way. The sounds of muffled moans imbue the otherwise quiet soundtrack. Steps. Searching for the young woman, he begins to open doors. Behind the first one he finds a couple having sex in the shower; he lingers watching before he catches himself and closes the door behind him. Is pulled towards the sound of women laughing; opens the door and finds a group of women in exquisite underwear making out, having sex, drinking champagne. One is sprawling in the bathroom with a pink vibrator next to her. Three women are fooling around in bed. A lady with a wide brimmed hat slinks up to him; they want to play with him too, but he excuses himself, smiles; then leaves them.

Behind the third door he gets the glimpse of an orgy of women and men together; startled, he shuts the door, takes a deep breath. A woman dressed only in burlesque underwear passes him in the quiet corridor; she kisses him on his cheek.

Behind the fourth door is an elegant little bathroom, dimmed lights, a tub surrounded by candles along one side, a glass wall along the other; he bumps his nose into it before discovering it. A soft teasing rhythm begins to play, and there she is, behind the glass wall. She rocks her hips to the music, loosens her belt; he smiles, rips off his jacket, goes all the way up to the glass. She unbuttons her dress, he his shirt, she lets the dress fall. He lays both hands on the glass, as if to help her with her corset; as if to kiss her. She dances suggestively, wearing only her red thong silk panties and her black stockings. Then she lies down, and with a hand within her panties, she begins to masturbate. He gets his hand down into his pants too and masturbates. Through crescendo, she comes; and he. The glass foggy, he stumbles back over into the tub; laughs. She blows out the candle on her side, the picture dims. In the last shot we see her walking up the stairs, out into the street. Fade-out.

Clearly, the women in these SoFilles Productions' films come across as sexually empowered; it is their wishes and initiatives that are fulfilled. From a sexual political perspective it is also interesting to see how these women take on the stereotypical male role (to have her fantasy to have sex with a stranger satisfied; to be the one who penetrates; to be the one who watches someone strip; to be the one who leaves afterwards). At the same time the scenarios are not along the simplistic lines of reverse feminism where women and men merely switch position; on the contrary, their sexual encounters are fundamentally about the equally mutual satisfaction of those involved.

The French pop artist Caroline Loeb (b. 1955) directed the first X-femmes film, "Vous Désirez?" (2008; You Wanted Something?), featuring the erotic fantasy of a woman as she discretely masturbates in a café while listening to her friend talk. In the abovementioned press release for their line of X-femmes films, SoFilles Productions comments on how fitting they see the introduction of X-femmes with a film that probes female fantasies and masturbation, meditating on "what provokes desire and pleasure," a question to which all the X-femmes films are devoted, as they note.[18] The film also stands out for its exquisitely charged energy of muted excitement.

The film begins with the two women in a café. They are both beautiful, classy and hip at the same time, wearing chic black leather jackets. One of them has dark wavy hair that reaches her shoulders, the other short ruffled blond hair. In the background hangs a painting featuring a lushly adorned slightly reclining woman; her lips form an enigmatic smile.

The women talk; smile, before all of a sudden the camera closes in on the dark haired woman's lips. Then the picture fades out.

At once we're in a dark apartment, in front of the same painting; we study it with the blond woman who holds a burning candle up in front of her. In the background is the muted sound of a woman's deep breathing. The blond woman follows the sound; we hear her quiet steps on wooden floors. She passes bookshelves along the walls of the corridor before arriving at a bedroom; burning candles imbue the room with a warm glow. Lying in a bed among brocade blankets in warm red earth tones, she finds the dark haired woman, wearing only thin transparent silk panties, a silk scarf over her shoulders, long pearl necklaces draping her. The woman is touching herself, masturbating. The blond woman whispers something to her, but except from the quiet sound of excited breathing, the room is otherwise completely still.

Beautiful close-ups capture the woman's chin, skin, breasts, nipples. She sneaks a finger down into her transparent silk panties, short soft hair beneath. The camera moves through gliding extreme close-ups, the picture almost indistinct; panties, scarf, pearls, fingers. The pictures fade in and out through an almost constant use of dissolving images.

Thin red curtains in the background emit a weak shimmer of sunlight, caressing her body. The blond woman kisses the dark woman's panties, pulls them down, then moves her hand over her naked body, slightly away from it; light energy radiates over the dark woman's skin. She lifts the dark woman's hand to her lips; gently licks it, sensually sucking her fingers. In floating interspersed cuts we see the shadows of their arched bodies on the wall.

The woman in bed fingers herself in a sexy sensual way, small discreet circles around clitoris alternating with a finger deep inside her. We hear the sound of her juices, her breath. She sits up towards the blond woman and erotically hand fucks a candle, her necklaces caress her rocking body until the blond woman blows out the candle, and nuzzles for a brief moment the other woman's face. Then the dark woman lies down again. Fingering herself yet again, reaching climax. Comes as the sounds bring us back to the café before the film abruptly cuts to her hand there, beneath the table, within her skirt, over her bare thighs and black knee stockings, still masturbating. A waiter approaches them; did they want something? No, thanks; we're fine, she smiles with blushing cheeks. In slow motion, the blond woman looks unknowingly up at the camera; the picture freezes here before it fades out.

"Le Beau Sexe" (2009; The Good Sex) by the prize-awarded French director Tonie Marshall (b. 1951) also depicts a woman's erotic masturbation fantasy. Or is what we see for real?

The film, while focusing on her desire and its escalation—from when she is home alone watching tango on the television, and then, aroused by the music and the dance, begins to masturbate, until she arrives at the apartment of a stranger who has called her with a sexual invitation—doesn't make this clear. The man who ostensibly calls her, presents himself as her neighbor, Vincent. He's not at home now, he says and gives her another address. But he tells her that he's been watching her for six months, he knows every detail of her body; he's awaiting her.

A flurry of images—of her, parts of his naked body, and the sex between the two—are spliced in between shots of her dashing off: with a trench coat on top, naked under-neath, long blond ruffled curls around her soft face, light feminine steps in elegant beige high-heeled sandals down the stairs. And all along while on her way, on the street, on the subway, she fantasizes about the man. She—and we—hear his voice only, describing their sex. We see his cock, his hands, his lips over her body; her riding him, her vulva enveloping his penis, fellatio, cunnilingus. The pictures flicker by while in the background is a calm, almost sinister music mixed with a Truffaut-ish tango. And as the tension and desire almost burst into climax, the camera rests on her face only as *her* voice gradually takes over from his. A soft glow imbues her face; her eyes are open at the camera, but her gaze is directed inwards. The film ends here.

Dirty Diaries: Government sponsored feminist cell phone art porn

Swedish documentary and experiential filmmaker Mia Engberg (b. 1970) has won fame around the world for her feminist porn film project *Dirty Diaries* (2009). For this collection, she invited several artists and filmmakers to make—with a cell phone camera[19]—their own feminist porn film, lasting a maximum of fifteen minutes. The result is twelve short films accompanied by a booklet where the women comment on their films.

As I mentioned, Mia received substantial government support for this project, in fact amounting to approximately eighty thousand dollars from the Swedish Film Institute. Conan O'Brien's "only in Sweden" sketch about it prompted the head of the Film Institute to write a letter to the cultural minister defending her decision. The Ministry of Culture has not interfered in the matter either before or after.

Prior to *Dirty Diaries*, Mia had gained a reputation as a producer of documentaries about society's outsiders, including gay skinheads, vegans, gender benders, and street kids. At one point, she was invited by Stockholm International Film Festival to make a short film with a cell phone camera. In response, Mia made *Come Together* (2006) featuring a number of women filming their own faces while masturbating.[20] Explains Mia:

The film was published on a web site and led to strong reactions. Many comments were negative, such as, "Hell, they look ugly. They could've at least put on some makeup."

I found the comments interesting. They show that we are still stuck in the old notion that a woman's sexuality should above all please the eye of the spectator — not herself.

I thought that those who reacted negatively to the masturbation scenes in *Come Together* probably needed to see more films in the same genre. To open their eyes. Consequently, I asked some artists, filmmakers and activists to make their own feminist porn film with a mobile phone camera.

The *Dirty Diaries* project was born.[21]

The women who contributed to the *Dirty Diaries* project made their feminist films according to a manifesto posted on the project's official website.[22] The manifesto dismisses beauty ideals (we're beautiful as we are); fights for women's right to be horny; rejects the good girl-bad girl dichotomy (sexually active and independent women are not either crazy or lesbian and therefore crazy); attacks capitalism and patriarchy (the porn industry is sexist because we live in a patriarchal capitalist society); encourages women to say NO when they don't want to, and YES when THEY want to; maintains the right to abortion; opposes censorship (it's impossible to change the way women's sexuality is portrayed if images in themselves are judged taboo); stands up against narrow gender categories; defends homosexuals and a sexual plurality; encourages the use of condoms and safer sex; and lastly makes a plea to others to make their own alternative porn: sexy films that women too can enjoy.

Testimony to the women's creative backgrounds, the films are all stylistically intriguing, in often unusual and surprising ways. Included are also films that disturb the viewer, reminding her our work for a non-sexist society is not done. These films also forces us to face a challenging question about how to "smash capitalism and patriarchy" without getting personal.[23]

As a whole, *Dirty Diaries* shows the potential of feminist porn as art to both move the viewer to feel and stir her to think and to act, sexually and politically. Each of the films reflects its director's reflective approach to her porn making, which is further underscored by what they say in the *Dirty Diaries* booklet. In the introduction, "What Is Feminist Porn," Mia sums up some key challenges that confront all women who set out to make their own alternative porn: "Is there such a thing as a female gaze and if so, what does it see?" and "How do we liberate our own sexual fantasies from the commercial images that we see every day, burying their way into our subconscious?" While each film varies distinctly from one another in content and in style—from the opening film's probing of the layers that separate us to others that explore our physical and emotional openings and the limits of our fantasies—they all reflect an aspiration "to see the world with new eyes," as Mia puts it.[24]

Each director's written commentary interacts with and speaks to her film. In my presentation of *Dirty Diaries*, I therefore include quotes from these narratives as they pertain to each film.

The short film collection is introduced by its musical leitmotif as credits in white capital letters flash over the black screen. To an upbeat rhythm, a woman compels you, repeatedly, to "get down on your knees!"

The title of the first short film enters, *Skin*, by Elin Magnusson (b. 1982), accompanied by dark almost menacing tones. Close-ups of two bodies intertwined on white sheets, both in beige bodysuits that cover literally all of them. Hands stroking. Softer notes are introduced in the music, muted sighs. A finger lingers on a crotch seam. The two kiss through their suits and we hear the sound of faint smacks. She pulls on his hard cock that protrudes from beneath his suit; there are wet spots on it around the top of his penis and lower belly. He presses his tongue out and makes licking movements towards her pussy. She does the same to his cock. Finds a scissor; cuts an opening for her mouth so she can actually lick the area of his penis. Cuts a hole for her eyes. And an opening by his neck; she teases a hand inside. Kisses the skin of his chest, down along his belly. Light crescendo in the music; giddy joy. He cuts a hole for his mouth and another for her pussy so he can lick it. Pulls a condom on two of his fingers; fingers her. The camera captures his fingers and tongue by her pussy closely to the sounds of licks, kisses, and now joyous drumbeats. Impatiently they pull their bodysuits off each other, their bodies intact, no cuts. They continue with

---

strokes, licks, kisses, and fingering, before she lies down on her back on top of him, his penis between her thighs, and she helps it inside of her. They kiss and the picture fills with their genitals, and the music turns into a more quiet melody with notes of anticipation, body against body, inside of body.

Whereas "Skin" dwells on "the hardened skin" of "old disappointments and badly healed wounds" that cause people their need for "help to remember the sensation of heat," here received with the aid of scissors that "rip up and get in," "Fruitcake," by Sara Kaaman (b.1983) and Ester Martin Bergsmark (b. 1982), circles in on the anus as an opening for connection. "There is an opening more greedy than the mouth," whispers a male voice in the background among heaving breaths. "It is never satisfied, you will end up there," the voice continues as shaky unclear close-ups float over the screen; an anus, or a tree stump, kiwi, plum fruit, a red rose. The camera never stops to clarify or give an overview; it just continues through restless trembling, some pictures clearer, others extremely pixilated. The camera returns to the bodies of a woman and a man, their buttocks and intertwined bodies. The sounds of someone chomping on a fruit, quick breaths, licks, kisses. The chime of an ascetic gong. An aggressive siren. A tongue licks an anus. The anus is penetrated by a finger, then a fist, a dildo, anal beads, butt plug, a rose. Cut to black.

"Night time" by Nelli Roselli (b. 1983) is described in the brochure as "straight sex filled with simple pleasure" in an attempt "to put the private into the public space, in order to erase the limits for what we are allowed to show and what we are expected to hide." A man and a woman kiss, smile, stroke and kiss each other. She fingers herself while kissing him impatiently and before giving him a hand- and blowjob. He comes in her mouth. He licks her pussy. Then she uses a little bullet vibrator on her clitoris; comes. All is shot without music and only accompanied by the sounds of their breaths, sucks, licks, and frantic moans. We hear the vibrator's vibrations, a dog barking in the distance, a cat purring. The lighting is dimmed and the cell phone shots appear almost filtered, the color is muted. The chaotic movements of the camera, and the unfocused and almost arbitrary feel of what we see, add more energy.

The next film is the DVDs only animated film: "Dildoman" by Åsa Sandzén (b. 1975). Surprising the viewer with its implicit message of the fatality in using others as sex toys, "Dildoman" first seduces the viewer with its esthetic capturing of female sexual pleasure in, ironically, a stereotypical men's club. We see men jerking off, their bodies drawn in white on black background, a psychedelic green wall in the background. The men are watching a woman on a billiard table being licked and fingered by another woman.

The film's main plot is introduced when a big pussy lowers itself down over an aging male customer's head, his bowed shoulders and potbelly. At first we only see big wet pussy drops splashing on his head before the pussy slides down over it, then all of him, making wet splashing sounds. In the next shot another woman helps to use him as a dildo on her. The man is naked except for his tennis shoes; an allusion to the porn cliché of naked bimbos wearing high heels to bed. Through image and sound we feel her pleasure, and he has a hard-on when she comes, but then kicks frantically with his legs against the contractions of her pussy, which, disturbingly, chokes and kills the little man. When he is pulled out, his head falls limply to the side, his dick hanging down. Cut to the opening picture outside, the sign is turned; closed.

The director's accompanying text suggests the scenario is based on a male client's "unusual request" but leaves it unclear what type of ending he requested.

"Body" Contact by Pella Kågerman (b. 1982) feels like women's payback time, getting back at men for reducing them to sex objects by doing the same to them in return. In her accompanying text to the film, Kågerman explains that she had for a long time wanted to make porn, but had not been able to find any men who would participate. Then on the website bodycontact.se, she and "Sofia" found "Lex Luthor." The film begins with an online video chat between Sofia and Lex. At one point Sofia asks to see his cock; he shows it to her. Does it look ok? he asks anxiously.

Sofia and Lex make a plan for him to come over to her place. In the elevator of her apartment building, she begins to kiss him, jadedly, while Kågerman films with the cell phone. He appears piteous: tall and skinny with a rain hat, beard and mustache. He wants to know who she (Kågerman) is, why she's there, why she's filming. He begins to stutter, seeming extremely nervous; wanting to leave. They hold him back; assure him the filming is just for them. He tries to relax, stuttering something about how this feels really strange, how he thinks it's sick. How he is feeling tricked.

The first part of the film focuses on the two women attempting to persuade the man to stay and let Kågerman film Sofia and Lex have sex. In the end, he gives in. But then he wants it to be good for *her* too; and he wants to impress the camera. Doesn't this feel good, he asks Sofia, aren't you glad I came? She looks neither aroused nor happy; she rolls her eyes to Kågerman filming as he keeps pumping and barking, trying his very best. The scene is empty and sad. The two ladies giggle behind his back when he leaves, mocking his bravura.

The feel of "Red Like Cherry" by Tora Mårtens (b. 1978) is quite different. The text that accompanies it criticizes porn's focus on "the naked act of fucking," explicit genitalia, and male ejaculation. Instead the director wants to capture the tantalizingly erotic quality of sensual details and what one does not see. Her film includes a series of close-ups spliced together in extremely fast tempo: an eye, a nipple, fingers stroking, water, sand, skin. The camera shoots in whirling fast motion. Close-ups so close that the images blur, teasing the viewer with the suggestion of skin, sheets, the contours of bodies coming together, sex. And we hear the sounds of waves, splashes, the dribbling of sand, sighs, moans, then ecstasy, and then finally breathing out.

"On Your Back Woman!" by "Wolfe Madam" portrays domination and submission between women, described in the text as "a violent yet tender comedy of five women finding the limit of their own empathy, pain and physical strength ... a burlesque dance of willpower, enticing us to explore the macho violence within female sexuality." In the opening sequence we are introduced to five women through snapshots to the sound of wrestling sport in the background. A gong resounds, a woman claps her hands, and then, in slow motion, they attack one another, two by two, throwing each other around in bed, trying to keep the other down, one on top; in a combat sport, smiling — or serious? Loud roars, from a wrestler—or a lion?—charge the shots. During intermissions from the slow motion filming, everything becomes real and everyday again. We hear the women breathing, sighing, and laughing. And then it's on with it again to the upbeat wrestling sport's music in the background.

"Phone Fuck" by Ingrid Ryberg (b. 1976) is one of my favorite Dirty Diary films. Exploring "the idea of longing and absence—and the tension between touching and not touching—as a trigger for desire," the film portrays phone sex between ex-girlfriends. The film crosscuts between each of the women in their respective homes on the phone talking tenderly with the other—they know it's best they're not together anymore, but each misses the other, and just wants to hear her voice—and the fantasy, or memories, they share in which they have sex together. The picture is electrified by the sound of their breathing, sighing, kissing, and licking. When they both begin to masturbate, their talk turns dirtier; to sexy stuff, about what they miss, what they used to do, are doing, when they have sex together. The film illustrates how words, and images, can move and arouse, for the two women, and for us watching. The quality of the cell phone camera's shots at times works as a retro filter over the pictures; it's esthetically successful, beautiful and intense. They come. Land. A nostalgic rhythm with strength and warmth accompany the credits.

"Brown Cock" by "Universal Pussy" is a celebration of "the pussy's fierce capacity to open, invite, receive and envelop" and the "brown cock" fisting her:" "We celebrate the brown cock and love that butches know how to use both hands and can please and film and talk at once. We continue to raise our fists in lust and struggle because we know that the best cock on the block can fuck girls senseless and say FUCK YOU to patriarchy at the same."

The opening shot sees a woman masturbating; she's helped by her partner to get her panties off before she fingers herself. She reaches for a dildo; gets help from her partner to pump it in and out while she continues to stimulate her clitoris. The camera captures solely her lower body throughout the film; we only see what's there, and what goes in and out, nothing else. A saxophone is playing in the background. Her clitoris becomes swollen, the labia wet from her juices. Her partner helps with her hand, penetrates with the dildo and her hand, then just her hand, her fist, her arm. The woman is pumped hard while she continues to massage her clitoris. Comes. We hear the two women speaking gently in low voices. I'm coming again, she whispers to her partner whose entire arm now is inside of her. And she comes again, shaking intensely. Before her partner again continues to fist her, fast, hard: the film intense to fade out.

"Flasher Girl on Tour" by Joanna Rytel (b. 1974)— a radical feminist video artist known for her performances of sexual flashing—picks up on the payback theme featured in "Body Contact." A semi-documentary, the film features a young woman performed by Rytel who gets turned on by flashing and masturbating in public, with a fuck you attitude towards men; even as she claims that she does not want do it "to take revenge on the patriarchy." Visually this film is interesting with its choppy cutting technique combined with an unfocused use of zooming, which adds an artistic filtered look. Rytel also uses the effects of an unsteady camera and quirky angles. But what fuels the film more than anything is the venom of her alleged lust.

In the voiceover that accompanies her film, Rytel bitingly recites her commentary. "I wanna expose myself to guys," she begins; old men, grown-ups, family fathers and other slobs." "Guy exhibitionists," on the other hand, she finds "all disgusting;" the only body parts men should be allowed to show publicly are boobs, she concludes, "cause I *love* male boobs."

The film features Rytel masturbating and flashing in public in several locations on a trip to Paris, including in a city fountain, on the metro, from the balcony of her hotel room, and more. She stops random men on the street and asks them to show her their tits. She goes to a sex club. Buys a dildo and checks out the porn on the shelves. Then puts on a harness with a bullet vibrator in her underwear. Heads out. Sits down on a bench next to an old fat man munching on his bagged lunch. She spreads her legs apart. Turns up the volume on the vibrator, moves closer; he leaves. She goes to a restaurant in a fancy hotel, finds a table. And, with the clitoris vibrator still in her panties, she turns up the volume at the moment when the waiter's butt is right in her view; she snickers. Returned to her hotel room, she flashes again on her balcony. Writes "flasher girl" with pink lipstick on the window, pulls down her lower lip, revealing the letters "on tour" tattooed on the inside of her lip. An aggressive rap music accompanies the credits.

Even as it plays on disobedience and punishment, "Authority" by Marit Östberg (b. 1976) captures a fundamental sense of mutuality that is absent from Rytel's film. The film portrays a bondage-game between two look-alike young Annie Lennox women who share "a violent understanding of lust," and for whom "sex is a dirty game, it's a threat, a promise. It's to be inside the limits of another person." One woman role-plays as a graffiti artist, the other as a cop. The film begins as the graffiti artist is caught red-handed by the cop. She tries to run away into an abandoned building. The cop catches up with her, but the artist immediately gets the upper hand. She ties the cop to a chair; spits at her. Pushes the chair over onto the floor, and gets the cop to lick her shoe. Finds a knife and cuts up the cop's pants by her crotch; takes a firm grasp of it. The *Dirty Diaries'* leitmotif melody with its happy-go-lucky beat and rhythmic "get down on your knees" sets in. The graffiti artist takes a break to smoke. Flicks off the ashes into the cop's mouth, has her swallow it. Then the two kiss. She gets the cop to lick her pussy; captured in raw, sexy close-ups. Comes. Opens the cop's shirt, kisses and fingers her before penetrating her anally with the cop's baton while massaging the cop's swollen pussy with her other hand. The cop comes. The two kiss again; smiling to one another. Now the cop is on the offensive. She handcuffs the graffiti artist and finger-fucks her hard from behind. The artist helps, rubbing her clitoris. We hear and see her juices on the hand of the cop pumping her, fast. The artist comes, and then again; harder. They both exhale deeply. Kissing intimately, they embrace.

In the final short film, "For the liberation of men" by Jennifer Rainsford (b. 1982), we're presented with dark fleeting images of stylized men's bodies in costumes and wigs. The text accompanying this film explains that it portrays an old demented woman's erotic fantasies. We see the glimpses of a wrinkled woman's face in the opening shots, the hand of an old person. Then the flickering shots of various men's legs dressed in women's stockings. A man in an elevator has a red wig and a blue dress on. Another man sits reclined in a leather chair wearing a yellow blond wig, a short fur jacket, blue stockings. A third man is in platinum blond curls, white lace stockings, nothing else; he's standing in an empty wardrobe. Eventually they all jerk off fervently, filmed in quick spinning shots; in the chair, in the elevator, in the empty wardrobe. The camera glides over a shimmering silver dress; the director explains that it was the dress she had the old woman wear for the shoot. In the final shots we see parts of the old woman's face again, an eye starring blankly into space. High monotonous surrealistic tones envelop the entire film, which leaves us wondering about the nature of our sexual fantasies and what provokes them.

Truly, what makes the *Dirty Diaries* collection so unique is "the range of inventiveness and the diversity among the films."[25]

Hardcore action and vanilla sex, queer and straight, flashing and fucking, provocation, penetration and poetry. The project is aiming to find new ways of expressing sexuality on film and to challenge our view on gender and erotica.[26]

Dirty Diaries received an Honorable Mention at the Feminist Porn Awards in 2010. Said the jury: "this film is diverse, edgy and an important contribution to the Feminist Porn canon."[27] It is also a truly promising indicator of what can come to be of creative feminist aspirations, when the inspiration of one woman's invitation is further bolstered by public state support.

Conclusion: What's in a Name

Though widely acclaimed, the *Dirty Diaries* collection has also received its share of criticism, and not only for its substantial state support, which caused controversy even within Sweden. While praising the films, several reviewers argued that the films were more about art than porn. Anti-porn feminists, on the other hand, held on to their stance that pornography is inherently objectifying. They therefore concluded that feminist pornography would constitute an oxymoron.

We've seen how the power of assumptions can affect even a well-intended filmmaker's attempts at re-visioning porn, in particular with respect to a couple of the Danish Puzzy Power films. I suggested a narrow notion of what constitutes porn might have prevented the director of the first Puzzy Power film to apply his proven talents towards a radical re-visioning of porn, a pity considering the intriguing quality of his earlier gender bending experimental films.

Exposing cultural assumptions and gender stereotypes for what they are, a growing number of women are today creating re-visioned feminist porn films that do not abide by a conventional understanding of "porn." Refusing men free rein in defining porn, several of these women claim, as we've seen, the "porn" word as a way to subversively change its meaning. In fact, their wide range of re-visioned porn films forces us to dismiss the question "at what point is it no longer porn" as entirely irrelevant as they radically transform what porn is all about.

* * *

Actually, there are today several sub-genres within women's re-visioned porn. New queer porn is for one intriguing for its endeavors to break down rigid gender roles while it embraces sexual fluidity. As a married heterosexual woman and mother of a toddler girl, however, I am even more fascinated by the new re-visioned porn that takes the "hetero" out of "~~hetero~~sexuality," breaking down gender roles as it too embraces a sexually fluid and democratic plurality. Hence the focus of my work and this book.

During my sabbatical in Oslo researching porn, a journalist who had interviewed me about my work, described the kind of porn I look at as "gourmet." In another newspaper, it was referred to as "humanistic." These labels are rather fitting, because obviously I don't like trashy fast food porn or discriminating and violent porn. I like porn that stands out for its high cinematic quality and for its strong progressive content.

At the "Good Porn" event I hosted, one young woman pointed out to me how much softer the porn I like is than the one by which she gets turned on: fetish porn where red monsters bite into women. In my presentation, I had briefly touched on the gender deconstructing potential of BDSM and fetish porn before continuing with the porn that interests me the most. And during the discussion, the therapeutic potential of fetishistic and extreme porn was brought up too; how some extreme porn can provide release for the user's individual tensions and fantasies triggered by psychological histories and cultural taboos, and thus function as a regulated space within which to explore and process these instead of turning to actual physical violence.

Regardless of a porn film's therapeutic potential, I simply cannot consider a porn film "good," however, unless it convincingly portrays the sex as consensual, pleasurable, and mutually desired. I also need to know that it was ethically made. In the case of the porn featuring red monsters biting into women, it was animated, so the issue of real people being physically violated is moot. Nevertheless: it is not showing consensual sex. Sure, it can provide an outlet for *something*, but as Ms. Naughty points out in a post about extreme porn, while one can "acknowledge that negativity may just be someone's fantasy ... surely we should be able to ask: what the hell is going on if you need hatred to get off?"[1]

Ms. Naughty gives the example of a looped flash video she'd come across online; a video advertisement for a porn site:

> The woman was "fish hooked" (had a finger in her mouth, dragging her head back at a painful angle), a penis was rubbed roughly on her face, she was choked and slapped. She also didn't seem to be enjoying herself much; her face was red and she was crying.

As Ms. Naughty notes, this is exactly the kind of extreme porn that Gail Dines discusses. In fact, from reading Dines's book *Pornland: How Porn Has Hijacked Our Sexuality* (2010), you'd think that almost all porn is like the extreme online gonzo she describes there, despite Dines' disclaimer as stated in her preface:

> I want to make clear that when I talk about "porn," I am referring mainly to "gonzo" — that genre which is all over the Internet and is today one of the biggest moneymakers for the industry — which depicts hard-core, body-punishing sex in which women are demeaned and debased."[2]

Escaping regulations by which even mainstream porn abides, the Internet is where you can find the gravest cases of extreme porn thankfully excluded from the shelves of even seedy mega sex shops.[3] But this point is lost on Dines' readers who go away thinking she's covered extensive ground. Dines adds to the confusion by devoting chapters on "the porning of our culture."[4] And by providing detailed numbers to describe the immense size of today's mainstream porn industry, including the amount of DVDs it releases each year: films that are not the subject of Dines' analysis.

There are indeed many problems with Dines' generalizations and theory, yet I agree with Ms. Naughty that we ought not dismiss Dines' concerns with the kind of content she addresses. Concludes Ms. Naughty:

> It seems reasonable to be asking questions about bad porn and extreme porn. We should be talking about what it means and how it affects us.

I'll say it again: the great thing about porn affecting us is that it can actually have a *good* effect on us. Re-visioned and transformed feminist porn proves my point. Re-visioned porn can change the way we think about and practice sex in positive ways, just as mainstream porn has affected the way we picture and practice sex in negative ways.

Even Dines considers the potential effects of what she calls a "counter-ideology" with which to combat the porn that is causing men to "use women and disregard them when done;" the porn that is turning men "critical of their partner's looks and performance;" the porn that lets men "see women as one-dimensional sex objects who are less deserving of respect and dignity than men, both in and out of the bedroom."[5] Muses Dines on such a "counter-ideology:"

> What do men need to be exposed to in order to counter the stories in porn? In media studies we ask similar questions when discussing how to immunize people to the constant flow of consumerist ideology that is paired with capitalism. Often the answer lies in providing people with a counter-ideology that both reveals the fabricated nature of consumer ideology and offers an alternative vision of the world. A counter-ideology to porn would similarly need to disrupt and

interrupt its messages, and it would have to be as powerful and as pleasurable as porn, telling men that porn's image of women is a lie, fabricated to sell a particular version of sex. This alternative ideology would also need to present a different vision of heterosexual sex, one built on gender equality and justice.[6]

Concludes Dines:

Few men are exposed to such a feminist ideology; rather, most men (and women) are fed the dominant sexist ideology on a daily basis to such a degree that gender inequality seems a natural and biologically determined reality. Porn not only milks this ideology for all its worth, it also wraps it up and hands it back to men in a highly sexualized form. In the absence of a counter-ideology, this pleasurable sexist ideology becomes the dominant way of thinking and making sense of the world. While porn is by no means the only socializing agent, thanks to its intense imagery and effect on the body, it is a powerful persuader that erodes men's ability to see woman as equal and as deserving of the same human rights that they themselves take for granted.[7]

I agree with Dines that it is high time we turn the beast of discriminating and demeaning porn on its head. Re-visioned porn by women is showing us how we can do that. In fact, re-visioned porn by women is the answer to Dines' plea for a counter-way of thinking about sex. A way of thinking that reveals the fabricated nature of mainstream porn as it offers an alternative, empowering, inspiring, and pleasurable vision of the world it depicts. One that is fundamentally based on gender equality and justice.

Dines laments that few men are exposed to such a feminist way of thinking about sex; that most men and women are instead fed the dominant sexist ideology.

But the women who create re-visioned porn, and the women and men who watch it are changing all of this.

There is no absence of a counter-way of thinking about sex: a bonafide counter-discourse for sex. But it is time we speak up for it. Because as Dines points out too: while porn is not the only socializing agent, it can be a powerful persuader in the way we conceive sex.

Porn is a loaded word. And porn holds a lot of power in how we perceive women and men as gendered, sexual beings. So picture a future in which the associations brought up by "porn" are positive and freeing rather than negative and coercing. Where the effects of porn in fact persuade us to see each other as categorically deserving of the same amount of respect and human rights regardless of our sex. Where the effects of porn are healing and empowering rather than degrading and constraining.

Re-visioned and transformed porn can help us get there.

Re-visioned porn by women already represents a real counter-weight to "porn" and pornified media. With our support, and I really believe this, it can fundamentally change porn as it's been known. And that will be a good thing for all of us, whether we're watching porn or not.

Afterword: Turned on by Porn

Perhaps after reading this book you'll find yourself inspired to watch some of the films, which is how I felt after reading film scholar Linda Williams' *Hard Core*. In the Appendix, I provide a list of women oriented sex shops that sell new porn by women, and film festivals that screen progressive porn. You can also find trailers and links to the films' online retailers at my website. Please visit me at annegsabo.com or go directly to my blog newpornbywomen.com.

Nielsen/NetRatings surveys have repeatedly found that women represent approximately a third of all online porn consumers. A new major international research project on people's everyday uses of porn (in any format) also quotes this number in a preliminary report, which furthermore reveals that younger women show significantly greater interest in porn than do older women, suggesting a generational shift that may eventually "reduce the overall differences between male and female interest in pornography."[1] In 2010, the UK-based edition of the women's magazine *Cosmopolitan* found that 60 percent of its readers have watched porn and an additional 14 percent said that they were open to the idea.[2]

Nevertheless, a "woman watching porn" is still surrounded by a lot of social stigmas. Even researching porn is not a neutral topic. I've received many awkward reactions, unwelcome solicitations, and unkind rejections from people when they find out about my work on porn.

Even fellow gender studies scholars have snickered at my porn research. A man—an internationally recognized American masculinities scholar—has behaved towards me as if I am ready for sex at any point, with any person.

While on sabbatical and researching feminist porn at University of Oslo's Centre for Gender Studies, I remember colleagues sheepishly asking after weekends and vacations if I'd watched any porn lately. The question everyone had on their mind but nobody dared to ask was if watching porn turned me on.

There's somehow something incorrect for a scholar to be turned on at work. But as Williams points out, the intention of porn is to stir a physical reaction, just as tragedies strive to induce tears, and horrors goosebumps.[3] In an updated version of *Hard Core*, Williams encourages us to think more about such visceral viewing experiences.[4]

The answer is yes; I often get turned on when watching porn. During my sabbatical, I preferred to watch it at home, after I'd returned from my office, or during weekends and vacations. I would watch it on the television or my laptop when working more intently, sometimes taking notes, other times just absorbing it, and on occasion masturbating.

It was shortly after my sabbatical that the man who is now my husband moved in with me. You know how it's so exciting to share everything about yourself in those first intoxicated days, weeks, and months of love? Well, for me, that included good new porn by women. Since my earlier experience watching porn with an ex boyfriend had been so uncomfortable, with my husband I started out by casually passing on to him a few films. Not feeling myself judged and noticing his positive reaction, I began to hang around on the couch while he was watching. My husband is really good at talking film and has a good eye for style, so we began discussing what we were watching. Just listening to him could turn me on. Then he even began to find stuff that he'd pass on to me, or invite me to watch with him.

We've since become parents of a toddler daughter who is not fond of sleep, so we haven't had the time to watch much of anything together, that is to say not just porn. In fact, since my daughter was born, I have watched a lot of porn at the college library where I go to write. Perhaps at home when she naps. I like finding short vignettes online or new trailers from some of my favorite porn makers, because I can actually squeeze those into my limited time.

If my husband and I have time together at night after our daughter is asleep, we often sit next to each other on the couch working on our laptops. Sometimes one of us will find a sexy short video that we can watch together, perhaps to consider featuring it at my online resource site Love, Sex, and Family, or at my New Porn by Women blog. Sometimes my husband will take a look at and comment on a film I'm writing about. And now and then this leads to more. In our case, though, the point is that we are able to integrate porn into our daily lives in a way that is meaningful to our work and to our sexual lives in general; we do not section it off as something that is forbidden or taboo, or in any way limited to utility and thus brought out of the closet at necessity. The kind of porn we watch is capable of inspiring us in a multitude of ways. This can be true for you too.

I was recently filling out a survey for the abovementioned international research project on the everyday uses of porn.[5] One of the questions was about what I would miss if I were not to watch porn in the future. I responded that I would miss the opportunity to see sexual imageries that can inspire new ways of thinking about and experiencing sex, broadening our minds and liberating more space to define and express our sexuality. And truly, one of the things that I find so stimulating about new progressive re-visioned and transformed porn is how it has that potential. The inspiration I have received from what I have watched of re-visioned porn is with me, even in those periods when I'm not watching a whole lot of porn.

Appendix

Featured filmmakers' websites

Candida Royalle (Femme Productions): *CandidaRoyalle.com*

Zentropa (Puzzy Power): *PuzzyPower.dk/UK*

Anna Span (Easy on the Eye):
Homepage: *AnnaSpansDiary.com*
Blog: *annaspansdiary.com/annaspansblog*

Jamye Waxman: *JamyeWaxman.com*

Abiola Abrams: *AbiolaTV.com*

Tristan Taormino: *PuckerUp.com*

Libido Films:
http://www.libidomag.com/shop/videos/videoindex.html (an incomplete list of the Libido Films at the *Libido* magazine's old, archived website).

Audacia Ray:
Homepage: *AudaciaRay.com*
Audacia Ray's new blog: *Blog.AudaciaRay.com*
Waking Vixen archived blog: *WakingVixen.AudaciaRay.com*

Petra Joy: *PetraJoy.com*

Ms. Naughty:
Louise Lush (Indigo Lush): *IndigoLush.com*
Blog: Ms. Naughty Porn For Women Blog:
www.msnaughty.com/blog

Ezine: For the Girl: *ForTheGirls.com*
Sex column: Grandma Scrotum's Sex Tips:
GrandmaScrotum.com

Erika Lust (Lust Films & Publications):
Homepage: *LustFilms.com*
Blog: *ErikaLust.com/Category/Blog*

Murielle Scherre (La Fille d'O): *LaFilledO.com*

Eva Midgley:
At Coco de Mer: *Coco-de-Mer.com/cococlub/erotic-film-collection*
Homepage/Blog: *EvaMidgley.com*

Anna Brownfield (Poison Apple Productions):
Homepage: *PoisonAppleProductions.com.au*
Blog: *AnnaBrownfield.Blogspot.com*

Jennifer Lyon Bell (Blue Artichoke Films):
BlueArtichokeFilms.com

Ovidie (French Lover TV):
Homepage: *Ovidie.net*
French Lover TV: *FrenchLover.tv*

Sophie Bramly (SoFilles Productions):
SecondSexe magazine: *SecondSexe.com*

Mia Engberg:
Homepage: *MiaEngberg.com*
Dirty Diaries: *DirtyDiaries.se*

Women-oriented sex shops

All of the below shops are founded by women, and each shop

features at least some of the films presented in this book, but none of them sell all the films featured. Please visit me at annegsabo.com (or go directly to my blog newporn bywomen.com) for a complete list of online retailers for each film.

United States and Canada

Eve's Garden. Founded in 1974 by women's rights activist Dell Williams, Eve's Garden caters to the discerning female consumer seeking to expand and celebrate her sexuality. The store is in the upper levels of an office building on New York's Westside, providing a discreet, comfortable atmosphere in which to shop. *119 West 57th Street, New York City, NY 10019, (212) 757-8651. EvesGarden.com.*

Good Vibrations. In 1977, dismayed by the lack of resources for women seeking accurate sex information and good sex toys in a well-lighted clean environment, sex educator Joani Blank opened the first Good Vibrations retail store in San Francisco's Mission District. Good Vibrations has expanded over the years, now running stores on each coast. Most recently, Good Vibrations was awarded Retailer of the Year (2011) by *Storerotica Magazine*, the national trade publication for the owners and operators of adult retail stores and lingerie boutiques. *GoodVibes.com.*

Babeland. Claire Cavanah and Rachel Venning opened the first Babeland store in 1993 in response to the lack of women-friendly sex shops in Seattle. Offering information and encouragement to women who want to explore their sexuality, the store has seen a steady growth in its popularity, leading to three more stores in New York, plus a thriving and educational website. *Babeland.com.*

Good For Her. Founder Carlyle Jansen got her start when she gave an impromptu sex toy seminar at her sister's bridal shower in

1995, and she's been sharing her knowledge ever since. Since its inception, Toronto-based Good For Her has refined its mission of giving women a safe place to shop, with "excellent materials that won't harm your body, and an approach to sex that gives you the ability to make the best decisions possible for yourself." Good for Her is the founder of the Feminist Porn Awards, which it has organized annually since 2006. *175 Harbord St., Toronto, Ontario, Canada M5S 1H3, (416) 588-0900 or (877) 588-0900. GoodForHer.com.*

A Woman's Touch. Founded in Madison, Wisconsin in 1996 by sex educator and sex counselor Ellen Barnard and physician Myrtle Wilhite, A Woman's Touch focuses on women's perspectives on sex and sensuality and is both an educational resource as well as a shop, promoting knowledge of sexual health, sexual education, and healthy pleasure. *600 Williamson St., Madison, WI 53703, (888) 621-8880. A-Womans-Touch.com.*

Venus Envy. Founder Shelley Taylor opened the first Venus Envy shop in 1998 and a second in 2001. These award-winning education-oriented sex shops and bookstores feature high-quality adult products and a wide range of books on sexuality and gender identity. Emphasizing that one of the best ways to enjoy a healthy and erotic sex life is to be informed, Venus Envy offers community events and workshops on sex and relation-ships in a safe, non-judgmental environment. Some of their workshops are for women only. *1598 Barrington St., Halifax, Nova Scotia, Canada B3J 1Z6, (902) 422-0004; 320 Lisgar St., Ottawa, Ontario, Canada K2P 0E2, (613) 789-4646. VenusEnvy.com.*

Early To Bed. Founded by Searah Deysach in 2001 to provide a safe space where women (and people of all genders) could shop for quality sex toys in a comfortable environment, Early To Bed is Chicago's first women-owned, women-oriented, boy-friendly, queer and trans-positive sex shop. Devoted to spreading its sex-positive message, Early 2 Bed carefully screens all their products and also offers workshops and talks on a wide-range of topics. *5232 North Sheridan Road, Chicago, IL 60640, (773) 271-1219 or (866) 585-2233. Early2Bed.com.*

Smitten Kitten. Founded in 2003, the Smitten Kitten has become a multiple award-winning institution in the Twin Cities. Its owner, Jennifer Pritchett, holds a graduate degree in Gender and Women's Studies, and has spoken about healthy sex toys and practices at colleges and universities. In 2005, Smitten Kitten launched the first-ever community advocacy organization and adult industry education organization, the Coalition Against Toxic Toys. *3010 Lyndale Ave S., Minneapolis, MN 55408, (612) 721-6088. SmittenKittenOnline.com.*

The Tool Shed. Opened in 2003 by a group of gals who felt that Milwaukee was in desperate need of a place that epitomized their beliefs about what a sex-positive, gender-positive, healthy and inviting sex toy store should be, the Tool Shed has since 2008 been in the reins of sex educator and writer Laura Anne Stuart. The Tool Shed focuses on safety and quality in the selection of their products, and provides a space where people of all genders can explore their sexuality in a comfortable environment. *2427 N Murray Ave, Milwaukee, WI 53211, (414) 906-5304. ToolShedToys.com.*

She Bop. Allied to create a boutique specializing in non-toxic toys, female-friendly DVDs, and gifts focused on sexuality, Evy Cowan and Jeneen Doumitt opened She Bop in Portland, Oregon in 2009. *909 N. Beech St., Portland, OR 97227, (503) 473-8018. ShebopTheShop.com.*

New Zealand

Sensual View. Not so long ago a group of friends got together for a "girl's weekend." As the wine and laughter flowed conversation turned to their more intimate relationships and how to keep the passion and excitement alive. Mainstream porn was given a scathing review. "Degrading, demeaning, offensive." "Where was the seduction and sensuality?" "What about erotic movies made for women?" These comments sparked the idea for Sensual View, a site focused on feminine fantasy and desire. *SensualView.co.nz.*

Europe

United Kingdom

Sh! Women's Erotic Emporium. 100% run by women who are passionate about providing the best service and advice for women and couples, Sh! Women's Erotic Emporium was established in London in 1992 as an antidote to sleazy sex shops. The DVDs Sh! sells are the softcore versions rated 18. *57 Hoxton Square, London N1 6HD, 020 7613 5458; 253 Portobello Road, London W11 1LR, 020 7221 5476. Sh-WomenStore.com.*

Coco de Mer. A luxurious women oriented erotic emporium, Coco de Mer was founded by Sam Roddick who opened the first Coco de Mer boutique in Covent Garden, London in 2001. Focusing on exquisite lingerie and designer toys and props made in consideration of the environment and human rights, Coco de Mer's online film collection features Eva Midgley's short erotic films. *23 Monmouth St, Covent Garden, London WC2H 9DD, 080 0011 6895. Coco-de-Mer.com.*

Sweden

Pistill. Founded by Tina Hagelin, Pistill opened the doors to its store in Stockholm in 2005. Offering a careful selection of products, Pistill seeks to be a source of inspiration for women and their health, sensuality, and inner well-being. *Drottninggatan 100, 111 60 Stockholm, +46 8411 6666. Pistill.se.*

Denmark

Lust Universe. Founded by Sabina Elvstam-Johns, the original Lust boutique opened in Copenhagen in 1998. A second store opened in Århus in 2006. Created for women by women with female sexuality as the centre of its attention, Lust is a tasteful and classy alternative to the traditional seedy porn shops. Lust also arranges events, lectures, private parties, and erotic photo sessions where women are invited to play with and explore their sexuality. *Mikkel Bryggers Gade 3A, 1460 Copenhagen K, +45 3333 0110; Vestergade 7, 8000 Århus C, Phone +45 8613 3022. LustUniverse.com.*

Norway

Flirt. Owned by NIE AS, the history of Flirt goes back to 1995 when the name for this Oslo-based store was Tanya's Playground and Tanya Hansen owned the shore. An erotic shop for women by women, Flirt focuses on delivering informed competence about their featured products, and has worked with health care professionals, local governments, and various foundations, including The Norwegian Association of Disabled, in order to support the sexual health and well-being of individuals who encounter challenges in their sexual life. *Møllergata 37, 0179 Oslo, +47 2236 1036. Flirt.no.*

Cupido. Though not female founded, Cupido deserves special mentioning as Norway's leading progressive sex-positive lifestyle magazine and online retailer. Launched by prize-awarded journalist Terje Gammelsrud as a special issue of his original holistic lifestyle magazine in 1984 (Cupido Shop followed in 1985, first via mail order and from 1998 also online), Cupido has gained a strong reputation for its careful selection of products, which includes quality toys and select films for women and men. I have been a member of Cupdio's team of contributing writers since 2006, and was most recently invited to take on the responsibility of screening and selecting all films featured in Cupido Shop. *Cupido.no.*

Netherlands

Mail & Female. Founded by Madeleine Vreekamp in 1988 in the infamous Red Light district in Amsterdam, Mail & Female is devoted to the positive experiences of sex, freedom, eroticism, and women's authentic sexual pleasures without all the clichés. *Nieuwe Vijzelstraat 2, 1017 HT Amsterdam, +31 2062 33 916. MailFemale.com.*

Female & Partners. Founded by Esther Suijker de Vries in 1994, Female & Partners is another Amsterdam-based erotic store for women focusing on quality, design, functionality, and fit in their selection of products. Run by women who confess to being "hopeless romantics who always have continued to believe in the power of love," Female & Partners hopes "to inspire you with our love for life and the primary source of energy, our sexuality." *Spuistraat 100, 1012 TZ Amsterdam, +31 2062 09 152. FemaleAndPartners.nl.*

Germany

Sexclusivitäeten. Founded by Dr. Laura Méritt in 1992, Sexclusivitäeten in Berlin features select high quality products purchased directly from their (primarily) female manufacturers and smaller enterprises to maintain the diversity of the market and to ensure products are made under ethical working condi-tions. Having since 2009 organized PorYes! Feminist Porn Film Award Europe, Sexclusivitäeten has for more than a decade also housed a weekly Friday afternoon "salon sexualis" where all interested are invited to discuss hot topics, watch and analyze porn, develop sex-positive educational campaigns, and more. *Fürbringerstr. 2, 10961 Berlin - Kreuzberg, +49 30 693 6666. Sexclusivitaeten.de.*

I invite you to visit Erika Lust's *Erotic Bible to Europe* online for more suggestions for shops in Europe: *EroticBibleToEurope.com.*

Progressive sex film awards and festivals

Feminist Porn Awards. Founded by the Toronto-based women oriented sex shop Good For Her, this awards festival has been organized annually since its inception in 2006. *GoodFor Her.com/Feminist_Porn_Awards.*

Berlin Porn Film Festival. Held annually in Berlin since 2006, this festival showcases new alternative porn. Spin-offs of the festival have been held in Athens, Paris, and Spain (different locations). *PornFilmFestivalBerlin.de/pff_e.*

CineKink. CineKink has been held annually since 2003 in New York City followed by national tours. The festival showcases sex positive films and videos that celebrate and explore the wide diversity of sexuality. *CineKink.com.*

Good Vibrations Indie Erotic Film Festival (GV IXFF SF). Debuting in 2006 as the Good Vibrations Amateur Erotic Film Competition at San Francisco's historic Castro Theatre, the competition became a full fledged Film Festival in 2008 with nationwide and interna-tional entries rounding out the winning entries. The festival offers an alternate forum for a broader exploration of "erotic cinema" beyond mainstream media. *GV-IXFF.org.*

Rated X: Amsterdam Alternative Erotica Film Festival. Held annually in Amsterdam since 2007, this festival seeks to address and reflect on the shifting, moving nature of the erotic in cinema, video, and other media. It embraces ambiguity in representation and welcomes a wide spectrum of genres. *RatedX.nl*.

Petra Joy Awards. Petra Joy first organized this award in 2009 in conjunction with Berlin Porn Film Festival. A second Petra Joy Awards was announced in 2012 with an entry deadline set at August 31, 2012. *JoyAwards.com*.

PorYes! Feminist Porn Film Award Europe. The Berlin-based sex educator and sex shop owner Dr. Laura Méritt first organized this award in 2009. A second PorYes! award ceremony was held in 2011. *PorYes.de* (click British flag for English language).

Circuito Off. Founded in 2000, this festival takes place during the first weekend of the main Venice Film Festival and has acquired a reputation as one of the most important video festivals in Italy and Europe. Circuito Off explores different genres within video creation, with special attention to experimental videos and the relationship between cinema and art, music and fashion. An "Erotic Night" was organized in 2008 and again in 2009. *CircuitoOff.com*.

Sexy International Film Festival (SIFF), Melbourne. Organized annually since 2008, this festival showcases quality films that explore love, relationships, and sexuality. A traveling festival, it opens in Melbourne, Australia and is followed by screenings around the world. So far, the festival has held screenings in Paris, New York, Los Angeles, San Francisco, London, and Perth. *SexyFilmFest.com*.

Sexy International Paris Film Festival (SIPFF). Created in 2009, this festival is the francophone version of the SIFF festival, focusing on Francophone content as part of its program. *SexyFilm FestParis.fr*.

Painted Lips and Lolly Licks. Organized annually since 2009 by the Ottawa-based non-profit arts and culture organization Apartment 613, this film festival showcases regional and international films that explore the erotic in unexpected, unprecedented, and non-exploitative ways. *OdessaFilmWorks.com/PaintedLips/home.html.*

Notes

Introduction.

1. Nielsen/NetRatings, a world leader in measuring Internet audiences, first reported this number in September 2003 when they found that 29 percent of all porn surfers are women. Several surveys from around the world, including by Nielsen/NetRatings, have since reported the same kinds of statistics for the consumption of porn.

2. Original title of this anthology is *Rosa Prosa: Om Jenter og Kåthet* (Oslo: Gyldendal, 2006). It has not been translated into English.

3. Original titles are *Sangen om den røde rubin* (Oslo: Gyldendal, 1956; first published in English as *The Song about the Red Ruby* in 1961 by Dutton, New York) and *Uten en tråd* (Oslo: Scala, 1966; first published in English as *Without a Stitch* in 1969 by Grove Press, New York).

4. I write more about these two novels and the cases against them in my article "The Status of Sexuality, Pornography, and Morality in Norway Today: Are the Critics Ready for Bjørneboe's Joyful Inversion of Mykle's Guilt Trip?" in *NORA: Nordic Journal of Women's Studies* 1 (2005): 36-47.

5. In my article "Highbrow and Lowbrow Pornography: Prejudice Prevails Against Popular Culture. A Case Study" in *The Journal of Popular Culture* 1 (2009): 147-61. As I here explain, the female protagonist of Bjørneboe's text invokes the rebellious spirit of the Ash Lad, who defeated the oppressive medieval power system and escaped his family's derision, as she defeats an oppressive moral code and escapes her family's repressive sentiments about sex. Espen Ash Lad is Norway's male version of Cinderella whose name in Norwegian is *Askepott*: literally "Ashpot."

6. Linda Williams also notes a prejudice among scholars

against lowbrow mainstream porn while in favor of high culture pornographic works, such as the novels of Marquis de Sade whose sadomasochistic texts explore such subjects as rape, bestiality, and necrophilia. See Chapter 1 in particular of her historical analysis of porn, *Hard Core: Power, Pleasure, and the "Frenzy of the Visible"* (Berkeley and Los Angeles: University of California Press, 1989).

7. *Hard Core* p. 232.
8. *Hard Core* p. 232.
9. *Hard Core* p. 247.
10. Bondage and discipline, sadism and masochism. "D" is also referred to as domination, as in domination and submission.
11. The event was co-hosted by Cupido, a leading sex-positive lifestyle magazine and retailer, and a national center for sexology.
12. Paraphrased from *Pornified: How Pornography Is Damaging Our Lives, Our Relationships, and Our Families* (New York: Times Books, 2005).
13. *Pornified* p. 275.

Chapter 1.

1. Pornographic texts and still pictures were first legalized in 1967, followed by the legalization of pornographic moving pictures in 1969.
2. *Uden en Trævl* (1968) was the film's original Danish title. The film was made by Palladium.
3. Quoted from Ariel Levy's *Female Chauvinist Pigs: Women and the Rise of Raunch Culture* (New York: Free Press, 2005), p. 68.
4. "Theory and Practice: Pornography and Rape," in *Take Back the Night: Women on Pornography* (New York: William Morrow, 1980), edited by Laura Lederer, p. 139.
5. Candida Royalle, *How to Tell a Naked Man What to Do: Sex Advice from a Woman Who Knows* (New York: Fireside, 2004), pp. xi-xii.

6. In her book *Reading, Writing, and Rewriting the prostitute body* (Bloomington: Indiana University Press, 1994), Shannon Bell provides a reconstruction of one of the *Deep Inside Porn Stars* performances based on its manuscript and interviews with Candida Royalle, Annie Sprinkle, and Veronica Vera. See Chapter 6 in particular.
7. Candida was married to Per Sjöstedt for nine years. They remained close after the divorce.
8. *How to Tell a Naked Man What to Do* p. xiii.
9. "Behind The Scenes," Candida Royalle (former website): http://royalle.com/scenes.aspx (last accessed December 1, 2005).
10. "Frequently Asked Questions," Candida Royalle (website): http://www.candidaroyalle.com (last accessed February 16, 2012).
11. Williams further describes the "money shot" as symptomatic of the porn genre's frenetic desire to represent the invisible, to capture pleasure in film; to make climax visible: "a substitute for what cannot be seen … a fetish substitute for less visible but more 'direct' instances of genital connection." *Hard Core* p. 95.
12. Gail Dines, *Pornland: How Porn Has Hijacked Our Sexuality* (Boston: Beacon Press, 2010), p. xxvi. Dines teaches sociology and women's studies at Wheelock College in Boston.
13. *Truth Behind the Fantasy of Porn: The Greatest Illusion on Earth* (Shelley Lubben Publications, 2010), p. 2.
14. Lilly Bragge, "Girls on top," *The Age*, June 16, 2004. Online: http://www.theage.com.au/articles/2004/06/15/108724491261 9.html (last accessed February 16, 2012).
15. Quoted from a former version of Candida's homepage. Archived online: http://www.candidaroyalle.com/femme faqs.txt (last accessed March 29, 2012).
16. Candida collaborated on these two films (both produced in

1984) with her co-founder of Femme Productions, Lauren
Niemi. The two went on to make Christine's Secret (also
produced in 1984; released in 1986), before parting on
friendly terms.

17. I provide a more substantiated discussion on women's re-
visioned porn as gender democratic discourse in my chapter
"A vision of new porn: – How women are revising porn to
match a time of greater gender equality," in *Generation P?
Youth, Gender and Pornography* (Copenhagen: Danish School
of Education Press, 2007), edited by Susanne V. Knudsen,
Lotta Löfgren-Mårtenson, and Sven-Axel Månsson.

18. *Going Too Far: The Personal Chronicle of a Feminist* (New York:
Random House, 1977), pp. 232, 235.

19. My translation quoting Aurdal's essay "Flink pike, free your
mind" (Good girl, free your mind) included in the aforementioned *Pink Prose* anthology.

20. *Hard Core* p. 251.

21. Natalie Angier, "Conversations/Ellen T.M. Laan; Science Is
Finding Out What Women Really Want," *The New York Times*,
August 13, 1995. Online: http://www.nytimes.com/1995/08/
13/weekinreview/conversations-ellen-tm-laan-science-is-
finding-out-what-women-really-want.html?pagewanted=
all&src=pm (last accessed February 24, 2012).

22. *Hard Core* pp. 251, 253.

23. "Behind The Scenes."

24. *How to Tell a Naked Man What to Do* p. 3.

25. "Don't portray me as a sexless grandmother," UK Film
Council (website), March 28, 2011: http://www.ukfilm-
council.org.uk/diversitystudy (last accessed February 16,
2012).

26. Originally an artist, Dodson (b. 1929) held the first one-
woman show of erotic art at the Wickersham Gallery in New
York City in 1968. She left the art world to teach sex to
women. She is widely known as a pioneer in women's, and to

a somewhat lesser extent men's, sexual liberation, having sold more than one million copies of her first book, *Liberating Masturbation: A Meditation on Self Love* (1974), which is richly illustrated by Dodson's own drawings. First self-published, the book has since been released under different titles, including *Selflove & Orgasm* (also self-published, 1983) and *Sex for One: The Joy of Selfloving* (New York: Three Rivers Press, 1996).

27. Attorney General's Commission on Pornography, *Final Report* (Washington D.C.: U.S. Department of Justice, 1986), vol. I, p. 78.

28. Justice Potter Stewart's statement, quoted from Williams *Hard Core* p. 283. See Williams *Hard Core* pp. 16-22 for more on the Meese Commission and the influences anti-porn feminists such as Robin Morgan and Andrea Dworkin had on it. Activist and writer Dworkin (who passed away in 2005) led the anti-porn feminist movement in the 80s together with lawyer Catharine MacKinnon. In her testimony before the Meese Commission, Dworkin alluded, on the one hand, to a series of photographs published in *Penthouse* magazine of Asian women bound and hung from trees and, on the other hand, to a *New York Times* article about the rape and murder of an eight-year-old Chinese girl in North Carolina whose body was left hanging from a tree. Concludes Williams: "Dworkin assumes a causal connection between the magazine photos and the crime, even though no evidence apart from the circumstances exist," p. 21.

29. Michael Scherer, "Debbie does Washington," *Salon.com*, November 10, 2005. Online: http://www.salon.com/news/feature/2005/11/11/porn_hearing/ (last accessed February 16, 2012).

Chapter 2.

1. Von Trier has won a reputation for his outspoken persona,

creating taboo-breaking and controversial films such as the Oscar nominated *Dancer in the Dark* (2000) starring Björk and Catherine Deneuve, a film for which he was awarded the prestigious Palme d'Or; the highest prize awarded at Cannes Film Festival. Other von Trier films worthy of mention include *Breaking the Waves* (1996, starring Emily Watson), which was bestowed the Grand Prix at Cannes; and *Dogville* (2003, starring Nicole Kidman), for which he was awarded another Palme d'Or. Von Trier was also nominated for a Palme d'Or for his most recent film *Melancholia* (2011, starring Kirsten Dunst and Charlotte Gainsbourg). Dunst won Best Actress for this film at Cannes.

2. Together with acclaimed filmmaker Thomas Vinterberg, von Trier wrote and co-signed the manifesto and its companion "vows" to purify filmmaking by refusing expensive and spectacular special effects, post-production modifications and other technical gimmicks. The two announced the manifesto at a cinema conference in Paris in 1995.

3. The manifesto was included in the original printed press kit for the first Puzzy Power film, and is now available online. "The Manifesto: Thoughts on women and pornography," Puzzy Power (website): http://www.puzzypower.dk/UK/ index.php/om-os/manifest (last accessed February 16, 2012).

4. Lisbeth's statement was included in the original printed press kit for *Pink Prison*, and is now available online. "The director speaks," Puzzy Power (website): http://www.puzzy-power.dk/UK/index.php/pink-prison (last accessed February 16, 2012).

5. *Hard Core* p. 276.

6. In 2008. In 2001, *Constance* was nominated for three AVN Awards: for Best Art Direction, Best Music and Best Videography.

7. Not including the gay Puzzy Power film *HotMen CoolBoyz* (2000) directed by Knud Vesterskov.

8. The film's working title is *Nymphomaniac*. Comments von Trier's producer Jensen to *The Guardian*: "This will also be a very amusing film too. A bit of fun, and slightly philosophical, following the sexual awakening of a woman." Ben Child, "Lars von Trier to offer softcore and hardcore versions of Nymphomaniac," *The Guardian*, August 2, 2011. Online: http://www.guardian.co.uk/film/2011/aug/02/lars-von-trier-softcore-nymphomaniac (last accessed February 16, 2012).

Chapter 3.

1. "About Anna Span," Anna's Diary (website): http://annaspansdiary.com/about_anna.php?pageno=2 (last accessed February 16, 2012).
2. Swedish porn scholar Magnus Ullén has suggested that the bad humor one can find in most mainstream porn is incorporated to provide the viewer with the means to detach from the porn he's watching, as in: "This is so incredibly bad, I can't believe my own eyes!" My translation quoting Ullén's article "'namnet för detta är ondska' [konsumtionssamhället och det pornografiska berättandet]." *bøygen* 4 (2005) p. 33.
3. 12.5 percent versus 5.2 percent. The data come from an extensive survey prepared for the Centers for Disease Control and Prevention (CDC) by CDC's National Center for Health Statistics (NCHS). "Sexual Behavior, Sexual Attraction, and Sexual Identity in the United States: Data from the 2006-2008 National Survey of Family Growth." *National Health Statistics Reports* 36 (2011). Available online in PDF-format: http://www.cdc.gov/nchs/data/nhsr/nhsr036.pdf (last accessed February 16, 2012).
4. Email to the author May 11, 2006.
5. "About Anna Span."
6. "Ideas on Sexual Politics," Anna Arrowsmith Liberal Democrat Candidate (website), April 14, 2010: http://

www.annaforgravesham.org.uk/articles/ideas-on-sexual-politics.htm (last accessed February 16, 2012).

7. "Ideas on Sexual Politics."

8. "First ever UK release of a film that contains female ejaculation," Anna Span's Diary (blog), October 5, 2009: http://annaspansdiary.com/annaspansblog/2009/10/05/first-ever-uk-release-of-a-film-that-contains-female-ejaculation/ (last accessed February 16, 2012).

9. John Ozimek, "Anna Span vs. the BBFC," *Eye for Film*, October 6, 2009. Online: http://www.eyeforfilm.co.uk /feature.php?id=736 (last accessed February 16, 2012).

10. Email to the author September 25, 2011.

11. "Porn debate to spice up Cambridge Union," *Cambridge News*, January 11, 2011. Online: http://www.cambridge-news.co.uk/Home/Porn-debate-to-spice-up-Cambridge-Union.htm (last accessed February 16, 2012).

12. Anna Span, "Historic Win for the Porn Industry at Cambridge Debate," *AVN*, February 21, 2011. Online: http://news.avn.com/articles/Historic-Win-for-the-Porn-Industry-at-Cambridge-Debate-426978.html (last accessed February 16, 2012).

13. Dan Damon, "Debate: Does pornography provide a 'good public service?'" *BBC: World Update* (radio), first broadcast February 18, 2011. Online: http://www.bbc.co.uk/world-service/news/2011/02/110218_pornography_debate.shtml (last accessed February 16, 2012).

Chapter 4.

1. See the Appendix for more details about Babeland.

2. *Fear of Flying* (New York: Holt, Rinehart and Winston, 1973), p. 14.

3. Dina Rickman, "Erica Jong On Feminism, Sex Addiction And Why There Is No Such Thing As A Zipless F**k," *The Huffington Post*, November 7, 2011. Online: http://

www.huffingtonpost.co.uk/2011/11/07/erica-jong-no-such-thing-as-zipless-fuck_n_1079222.html (last accessed February 16, 2012).

4. Erica Jong, "Is Sex Passé?" *The New York Times*, July 9, 2011. Online: http://www.nytimes.com/2011/07/10/opinion/sunday/10sex.html (last accessed February 16, 2012).

5. "Official Biography," Abiola Abrams (website): http://abiolaabrams.com/about_abiola.html (last accessed February 16, 2012).

6. The magazine was published from 1988 until 2000. Some of the content is archived online at libidomag.com.

7. "Recent News," Candida Royalle (website): http://www.candidaroyalle.com/recentnews.html (last accessed February 16, 2012).

8. Email to the author December 2, 2009.

9. For couples wanting to make their own erotic home movie, Joy wrote the book *Make Your Own Adult Video: The Couple's Guide to Making Sensual Home Movies, from Setting the Scene to Making the Scene* (London: New Holland Publishers, 2006). Petra dissolved her Strawberry Seductress company after the release of *Feeling It!* and now releases all her films under the Petra Joy label.

10. "Frequently Asked Questions," Petra Joy (website): http://www.petrajoy.com/faq.asp (last accessed February 16, 2012).

11. "About Petra," Petra Joy (website): http://www.petrajoy.com/vision.asp (last accessed February 16, 2012).

12. "Frequently Asked Questions."

13. "Frequently Asked Questions."

14. It is, however, legal to make and sell porn in the territories (which officially aren't states). This means that, before the Internet, Australians bought all their porn videos from Canberra in the Australian Capital Territory, officially Australia's seat of government.

15. Email to the author April 12, 2006.

16. "About Us," Indigo Lush (website): http://www.indigolush
.com/aboutus.html (last accessed February 16, 2012).

Chapter 5.

1. With her first two collections, *Femme* and *Urban Heat*, which
were both produced in 1984 and released in 1985.
2. Erika Lust, *Good Porn: A Woman's Guide* (Berkeley, Seal Press,
2010), pp. 6-7.
3. Ariel Levy, *Female Chauvinist Pigs*, p. 186. Melinda Gallagher
and Emily Scarlet Kramer, *A Piece of Cake: Recipes for Female
Sexual Pleasure* (New York: Atria Books, 2005), p. 180.
Gallagher and Kramer launched the CAKE movement in
2000 in New York City. Criticized by Levy as another
example of today's raunch culture of women naively seeking
empowerment by flaunting as sluts and sex objects, CAKE
was organized as a series of women's sex parties (men
allowed if accompanied by a female) where women were
encouraged to explore and enjoy their body and sexuality,
including by pole dancing and stripping. The movement
spread to San Francisco and also took off in London. The last
documented CAKE party took place in the fall of 2007.
4. "The Heroine of this Vampire Film is Woefully Anemic," *The
Independent*, September 7, 2008. Online: http://www.
independent.co.uk/arts-entertainment/books/reviews
/breaking-dawn-by-stephenie-meyer-917865.html   (last
accessed July 15, 2011).
5. Emphasis hers. "Twilight or 50 years back in time," Erika
Lust (blog), June 30, 2011: http://www.erikalust.com
/2011/06/30/twilight-or-50-years-back-in-time/ (last accessed
February 16, 2012).
6. "Erika Lust on making porn for women," *Filament*, May
2011. Online: http://www.filamentmagazine.com/2011/05
/erika-lust-on-making-porn-films-for-women/ (last accessed
February 16, 2012).

7. The Poetry Brothel was launched in January 2008 by Stephanie Berger (aka the Madame) and fellow New School MFA graduate Nicholas Adamski (stage name Tennessee Pink). From The Poetry Brothel's webpage: "The Poetry Brothel, a unique and immersive poetry experience, takes poetry outside classrooms and lecture halls and places it in the lush interiors of a bordello. The Poetry Brothel presents poets as high courtesans who impart their work in public readings, spontaneous eruptions of poetry, and most distinctly, as purveyors of private poetry readings on couches, chaise lounges and in private rooms. Central to this experience is the creation of character, which for poet and audience functions as disguise and as freeing device, enabling The Poetry Brothel to be a place of uninhibited creative expression in which the poets and clients can be themselves in private. The Poetry Brothel also explores and responds to the tendency of poets to undervalue themselves inside the creative marketplace by providing a seductive and intimate means of confirming for writers and audience alike the literal monetary value of such work." "About The Poetry Brothel," The Poetry Brothel (website): http://www.thepoetrybrothel.com/ (last accessed February 16, 2012).

8. All were originally published in Spanish as *Porno Para Mujeres* (2008), *La Biblia Erótica de Europa* (2010), and *Deséame como si me odiaras* (2010).

9. The manifesto ("La Fille d'O? La Fille d'O!") is available online in PDF-format: http://www.lafilledo.com/media/pdf/manifest.pdf (last accessed February 16, 2012). Murielle here asserts "a thorough love for the human body" while she rejects airbrushed or "touched up" pictures, as she calls them. "We select our models not just with the eyes but with all our senses," she writes. She also stresses that her lingerie is "practical" and therefore does not come in sets of same size, because "same size top and bottom bodies are just not

as common." Working with high quality fabrics and handmade designs, she opposes outsourcing and the marketing strategy of branding collections according to seasons. "A new collection comes out when it's done. Not when it is supposedly best released, from a commercial point of view."

10. Raindance was founded in 1992 by filmmakers, for filmmakers, launching year round training courses that same year. Its courses have been attended by several prestigious filmmakers.

11. Louise Bak, "Fantasy Quickies," *Toro Magazine*, July 28, 2009. Online: http://www.toromagazine.com/?q=node/2025 (last accessed February 16, 2012).

12. A matryoshka doll, also known as a babushka doll, is the name for a Russian doll where a set of dolls of decreasing sizes are placed one inside the other.

13. "Fantasy Quickies."

14. "Fantasy Quickies."

15. "The Winners," Shooting People (website): http://shooting-people.org/destricted/winners.php?over18=true (last accessed February 16, 2012).

16. "Fantasy Quickies."

17. "Fantasy Quickies."

18. Email to the author October 29, 2009. In yet another email, Eva added this: "Without Sam Roddick though, none of the films would have happened. Sam is a major creative force, she is always bubbling over with ideas and a very inspiring person all over. I owe her" (email to the author March 1, 2012).

Chapter 6.

1. Quoted from "About Hungry Films," Hungry Films (website): http://www.hungryfilms.com/hungry.htm (last accessed December 1, 2009). Brownfield co-founded Hungry

Films for the production of *The Band* with her co-producer Aer Agrey (b. 1979). The Hungry Films website is no longer active, but all the information can be found on Hungry Film's Facebook page: http://www.facebook.com/pages /Hungry-Films/205585102820733?sk=info (last accessed February 16, 2012).

2. Kelli Armstrong, ed., "Sisters are doin' it for themselves!" *Cleo*, June 2004, p. 134.

3. Michael Lallo, "People assume feminist means lesbian," *The Age*, March 3, 2008, p. 16.

4. "Welcome to Blue Artichoke Films," Blue Artichoke Films (website): http://blueartichokefilms.com/ (last accessed February 16, 2012).

5. For an *Amsterdams Peil* episode directed by Rogier Timmermans for channel AT5. This television special on Blue Artichoke Films is included as an extra on the DVD of Jennifer's film *Matinée* (2009).

6. *Amsterdams Peil*.

7. "About Blue Artichoke Films," Blue Artichoke Films (website): http://blueartichokefilms.com/about/ (last accessed February 16, 2012).

8. *Amsterdams Peil*.

9. Andrew Hussey, "Liberty, fraternity, pornography. Why Ovidie made French porn a political issue," *The Times Magazine*, January 18, 2003, p. 35.

10. Ovidie, "My porn manifesto," *The Guardian*, April 12, 2002. Online: http://www.guardian.co.uk/film/2002/apr/12/arts features (last accessed February 16, 2012).

11. "An innovative concept," French Lover TV (website): http://www.frenchlover.tv/tv/content.php?rub=12&id_rds=1 03 (last accessed February 16, 2012).

12. "An innovative concept."

13. "Chicks with Guts," Porn Film Festival Berlin 2009 Program. Online: http://www.pornfilmfestivalberlin.de/pff/?page_id

=397 (last accessed February 16, 2012).

14. SoFilles Productions, "X-Plicit Films: As close as possible to women's desire," released in October 2008 after the fall premiere of *X-femmes*. Also mentioned in the press release, in addition to the Oscar awarded film *The Piano Lesson* (1993) by the New Zealand director Jane Campion, are the French films *Lady Chatterley* (2006) by Pascale Ferran and *Le Bal des Actrices* (2009) by Maïwenn Le Besco.

15. Lizzy Davies, "Paris intellectuals make case for porn," *The Observer*, October 12, 2008. Online: http://www.guardian .co.uk/film/2008/oct/12/france-festivals (last accessed February 16, 2012).

16. Media Group TV, *Giuria / Jury: Sophie Bramly @ Circuito Off 09 Day 02* (video). This interview was done in conjunction with Cirquito Off (2009). Online: http://www.vimeo.com/6533324 (last accessed February 16, 2012).

17. Elaine Sciolino, "France. Sex. Problem?" *The New York Times*, October 29, 2008. Online: http://www.nytimes.com/2008/10/30/fashion/30cliente.html?pagewanted=all (last accessed February 16, 2012).

18. "X-Plicit Films."

19. Exceptions were made for two of the short films, one of which is the animated computer produced film. The other is "Skin," which was shot with a high-definition video camera because, explained Mia to me in an email, the cell phone camera was unavailable the day this film was shot.

20. *Come Together* is included as an extra on *Dirty Diaries*.

21. Mia Engberg, "What Is Feminist Porn?" Introduction to the *Dirty Diaries* booklet.

22. http://www.dirtydiaries.se/ (last accessed February 16, 2012).

23. "Manifesto," Dirty Diaries (website): http://www.dirtydi-aries.se/ (last accessed February 16, 2012).

24. "What Is Feminist Porn?"

25. "What Is Feminist Porn?"

26. "Films," Mia Engberg (website): http://www.miaengberg. com/ (last accessed February 16, 2012).
27. "The Fifth Annual Good For Her Feminist Porn Awards 2010," Good for Her (website): http://goodforher.com/fpa _2010. *Dirty Diaries* also won a PorYes! Feminist Porn Film Award Europe (2011).

Conclusion.
1. "Let's Talk About Extreme Porn," Ms. Naughty Porn For Women (blog), March 4, 2011: http://www.msnaughty.com /blog/2011/03/04/lets-talk-about-extreme-porn/ (last accessed February 16, 2012).
2. *Pornland* p. xi.
3. At least in the US, this is the case for the Internet. Pamela Paul points out that other countries have taken measures to fight back, including Norway where a nationwide child pornography filter on all Internet access has been introduced (*Pornified* pp. 191-92).
4. *Pornland* p 163.
5. *Pornland* p 98.
6. *Pornland* p. 98.
7. *Pornland* p. 98.

Afterword.
1. This extensive research project is led by three UK-based researchers: Clarissa Smith, Feona Attwood, and Martin Barker. Their preliminary report ("Pornresearch.org: preliminary findings," October 2011) is available online in PDF-format: http://www.pornresearch.org/Firstsummaryforweb site.pdf (last accessed February 16, 2012), p. 3.
2. Cosmo Team, "The Cosmo sex survey results are in!" *Cosmopolitan UK*, June 9, 2010. Online: http://www. cosmopolitan.co.uk/love-sex/tips/the-cosmo-sex-survey-results-are-in-101510 (last accessed February 16, 2012).

3. *Hard Core* p. 5.
4. *Hard Core* (1999) p. 289-92.
5. The project's survey is now closed. More than 5,000 people filled out the survey. Responses are currently being analyzed. Results will be presented and published in a variety of ways, and a digest of the main findings will be posted at the project's website: http://pornresearch.org/ (last accessed February 16, 2012).

Anne G. Sabo is a former academic turned public educator, author, speaker, freelance writer, and mama- and sex blogger. As a college professor, she taught courses in literature, film and women's studies. She has researched feminist pornography for more than a decade and has become an acknowledged expert in the field. She has written numerous articles and essays on the subject, and is a frequently consulted speaker on the topic. She grew up in Norway, earned her Ph.D. from University of Washington, and lives in Northfield, Minnesota with her husband and their toddler daughter. You can visit her at annegsabo.com.

Contemporary culture has eliminated both the concept of the public and the figure of the intellectual. Former public spaces – both physical and cultural – are now either derelict or colonized by advertising. A cretinous anti-intellectualism presides, cheerled by expensively educated hacks in the pay of multinational corporations who reassure their bored readers that there is no need to rouse themselves from their interpassive stupor. The informal censorship internalized and propagated by the cultural workers of late capitalism generates a banal conformity that the propaganda chiefs of Stalinism could only ever have dreamt of imposing. Zer0 Books knows that another kind of discourse – intellectual without being academic, popular without being populist – is not only possible: it is already flourishing, in the regions beyond the striplit malls of so-called mass media and the neurotically bureaucratic halls of the academy. Zer0 is committed to the idea of publishing as a making public of the intellectual. It is convinced that in the unthinking, blandly consensual culture in which we live, critical and engaged theoretical reflection is more important than ever before.